**BERNARD GITTELSON'S OWN LIFE PROVES
THAT HIS SUCCESS FORMULA
CAN WORK AGAIN AND AGAIN . . .**

—By age 22, he served on New York State Legislature
  Committees and was instrumental in getting
  the first anti-discrimination law passed.

—He created:

  • the first college on Labor and Industrial Relations
  • computerized astrology
  • the biorhythm business

—His public relations firm won accounts such as
  the West German government and the European Common
  Market after only three years in business.

—He has sold millions of books and writes a
  world-wide syndicated column.

—His products and services have made him one of the
  top consultants in U.S. industry.

Read Bernard Gittelson's inspiring
true stories
and maybe you, too, can create
your own luck!

Books by Bernard Gittelson

Biorhythm: A Personal Science

How To Make Your Own Luck

Published by
WARNER BOOKS

Bernard Gittelson

How to Make Your Own Luck

WARNER BOOKS

A Warner Communications Company

WARNER BOOKS EDITION

Book design by H. Roberts Design

Warner Books, Inc., 75 Rockefeller Plaza, New York, N.Y. 10019

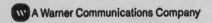 A Warner Communications Company

Printed in the United States of America

First Printing: November, 1982

10 9 8 7 6 5 4 3 2 1

This book is dedicated to the memory
of my mother and father.

Whatever you can do or dream you can do,.
begin it.
Boldness has genius, power and magic
in it.

—GOETHE

Contents

Preface

I am going to teach you how to be lucky. That's a promise. It may take years to become rich or famous or to achieve your ultimate goal in life. Only *you* can bring that about. It would be silly to pretend this book can do it for you.

What I do promise is this: If you'll absorb what I'm about to tell you, and carry out the simple steps outlined in the chapters that follow, you can improve your financial status, lead a more exciting, satisfying life, and raise yourself to a new level of success.

I was on a plane leaving Tokyo, having just sold the Sony Corporation the rights to my biorhythm computer program, when I started to read Milton and Rose Friedman's book *Free to Choose.* I found myself musing as much about the author himself as about what he had to say.

Here was a man who had won the Nobel prize, had a book on the best-seller list, and was the star of his own television series on economics—a celebrity in the spotlight;

yet I knew of a dozen other brilliant and equally qualified economists who haven't earned a fraction of the money Friedman has or made anywhere near as much impact.

What a lucky guy, I said to myself, to be enjoying so much success. Every week you hear him quoted or run across something he wrote. Suddenly I had another thought: Lucky, *hell.* All that success didn't just happen. He *made* it happen. This guy made his own luck. The idea seemed a revelation. As I thought more about it, I took out a pad and started to jot down random items: *Luck.* Just what is it, exactly? Can you make your own luck, and how do you make it? I also started to reflect on the "lucky breaks" I had brought about in my own life.

Although my parents were poor immigrants—not the kind to have powerful connections—at twenty-one I was already working on legislative committees. I traveled across the country with then Senator and later Vice President Alben Barkley, making speeches and raising money. In 1951 my public-relations firm, though only three years old and with three employees, succeeded in landing the West German government account. Later I advised the European Common Market, opened trade centers in England and Europe for the U.S. Department of Commerce, and helped launch Operation Bootstrap for Puerto Rico. I also organized the press conference that introduced both the Volkswagen and Mercedes automobiles in the United States, helped launch the Cerebral Palsy and Muscular Dystrophy associations by running their first press conferences and giving other assistance in their first year, and on numerous occasions counseled heads of government and leaders of industry all over the world.

Am I lucky? Lots of people say so. Yet I know it's not luck at all—I've worked my ass off for the last forty years.

I like it when people ask me about myself. I like answering such a question as How does a three-year-old PR firm land a million-dollar account? Or, How does a relatively inexperienced firm convince the West German government that it can be helped by their advice when the head of the firm is only a kid in his twenties and a Jew at that? The answers are so simple. I got the account by writing a letter and asking for it. They sure needed PR. A former enemy country that affected millions. They didn't need publicity; they needed sensitive guidance—especially in the beginning, when it was so easy to make mistakes.

Twenty years ago I was decorated by the West German government, and with this decoration they issued the following proclamation:

ADDRESS
by German Ambassador Wilhelm G. Grewe
at a ceremony in honor of
MR. BERNARD GITTELSON
in Washington, D.C., May 3, 1961

Gentlemen,

We are looking back today on ten years of fruitful and loyal cooperation between you and the Federal Government of Germany. When you started to work with us and to advise us on how to further understanding between the American and German people the memory of the horrors of World War II were much move vivid than today and public relations as a means to improve relations between nations was a concept rather foreign to the German government and its representatives in this country. For both these reasons the job you have done was a pioneer's job.

The standing, reputation and efficiency of your Public Relations Company is an established one in such a way that I need not go into any details praising them or the accomplishments. We are, however, deeply grateful for the advice we enjoyed and the assistance you provided.

It would not be fair not to mention that you also convinced us that public relations is no wonder drug which, after application, makes black look white and vice versa. You have helped us to understand how much diligent day-to-day work is involved and necessary to improve the image one nation has of another even by inches or shades.

You, in your own particular field of action, have throughout these ten years done much more than what your contract with the German government asked of you. I gratefully recognize today that these your efforts have only one explanation: your conviction that an incalculable contribution to peace and freedom in this world of ours is made by a reconciliation between the American and German nations and by establishing close bonds of friendship and understanding between them.

In recognition of your unrelenting and loyal efforts in this field the President of the Federal Republic of Germany has bestowed upon you the Commander's Cross of the Order of Merit of the Federal Republic of Germany which I have the honor and pleasure of handing over to you.

Of course, not all the good things that happened to my clients were the result of my public-relations counseling. They had advice from many other sources, and they were wise enough to know which ones to follow. I am sure many of my suggestions were turned down, and rightly so. Nevertheless, I think I can honestly claim to have been right much more often than wrong, not because I was especially brilliant but because I was down to earth, level-headed, and believed progress was made step by step. Anything that loomed up too fast tended to alarm me and put me on guard because, like a rubber band, it could snap back faster than one could expand it.

Over the years I have come to realize how certain principles have governed my life, and I have also become aware of how these same principles have played their part in the lives of others. My idea in writing this book is to tell you how you, too, can apply those principles, and apply them successfully. They will work for you just as well as they have worked for everyone else who has made his or her way up the ladder, no matter how heavy the odds may seem at this moment.

Do I hear you saying you're physically handicapped? Born on the wrong side of the tracks? Too young or too old? Lacking in education or experience? Your IQ is unimpressive and no one would turn around to give you a second look? You've already failed twice or three times or even more, and are ready to call yourself a born loser? It's not in the cards for you to succeed because they're stacked against you? It's too late now to make anything out of your life?

Well, then, this book is for you. I will demonstrate to you how I did it—how many famous people did it, how many people who aren't famous but *are* highly successful did it—and how you can do it, too.

No doubt you've seen ads for those books that purport to tell you how to make a million in real estate, or how to earn $100,000 in your spare time, or the easy way to become a millionaire. Well, I doubt if any reader of those books ever became rich, though I dare say the authors did very well. The notion that there's any easy road to wealth or success may sound good, and it may even hold true for a handful of people; but for most people the way up is never easy—success comes hard. The real thrill in life comes from bettering yourself bit by bit through your own efforts and by helping others at the same time.

I don't promise you millions or even hundreds of thousands of dollars. I do promise to show you how—by making others' lives more livable—you can make more money than you're now making (regardless of the amount), or how to make money for the first time, or how to make it when every door seems to be closed.

I promise you the thrill that comes when you open your eyes and use whatever knowledge you now have to become aware of the opportunities lying all around you—and when you are inspired enough to do something about them.

Luck involves aggressively overcoming obstacles. It means becoming aware of the particular gifts that you as an individual possess, which are really untapped natural resources. It also means perseverance. I've read that the Amazon River basin in Brazil is the richest in natural resources in the world—yet its people are among the world's poorest. Riches of any sort—personal or geological or environmental—must be tapped and used, or they might as well not exist.

You are going to have to help yourself. No book ever written can pull or push you to success; it can only point the way. You yourself must decide that you want to succeed, economically and otherwise, and then act accordingly.

If you wish to sit on top of a mountain and contemplate nature and think beautiful thoughts, fine—do so. That's your choice. But if you want to succeed in our crassly material world, if you want to live better and help others around you live better, then you'd better start making your own luck right now.

No excuses, mind you. I've heard them all, and none of them holds water. If people have learned to paint who have no arms, if people have achieved success at eight or eighteen or, for that matter, at sixty-eight or seventy-eight, if people have succeeded after many failures, then *you* can succeed. If you will open your eyes, relate to other people, remember what you see, hear what is going on all around you, and use your common sense, then you already possess a million-dollar research laboratory—namely, *yourself*—that can turn out all the ideas you need to take you to the top. Look, read, and listen with the purpose of asking yourself, How can I *benefit* from what I read, see, and hear? How can I be helped by people I meet casually, or in school, or in business, or even at church or community functions? Your best contacts are the people you've already met.

Lack of capital needn't hold you back, either. Sony, one of the world's leading electronics firms, was started with four hundred dollars. That great mail-order house, L. L. Bean, was started with a borrowed five hundred dollars. England's largest department-store chain, Marks & Spencer, was started by the present manager's grandfather, an immigrant from Poland who set up shop with little more than the slogan "Don't ask the price—it's only a penny."

Many people have succeeded by investing a large amount of money in a franchise, relying on a famous name or an unusual product as a means of achieving business success. But remember that even the most popular franchise is only a license to make money, not a guarantee. The holder still has to work hard, often day and night, frequently seven days a week.

In any case, this book is not intended for those who already have money to invest in order to make still more money, although it may give them some ideas they never thought possible—even for them. This book is intended for the kind of person who can sense what other people need and then rouse enough enthusiasm within himself to do something about it. That kind of person doesn't need money as a magic talisman to get him started; he can carry out his ideas successfully with guts and hard work alone.

Remember that people are susceptible to enthusiasm. If you have it, you can turn those around you into eager customers of whatever product or service you have to offer. That kind of enthusiasm comes from knowing exactly what you're doing, which you'll learn in this book. And I must tell you right now that it's the very life blood of all your efforts.

To embark on any project without such motivation is like starting out in a car with no gas. You won't get far. But with it, nothing on earth can stop you from achieving success.

There is no easy way to riches, but there is a pretty sure way if you are reasonable and determined, two virtues most of us have. Let's even use our faults to advantage.

You are about to learn the chemistry of luck.

BERNARD GITTELSON

New York City

How to Make Your Own Luck

1

Let's Get Acquainted

When you bought this book, you and I automatically formed a partnership—a mutual undertaking aimed at improving your luck. But partnerships can work effectively only to the extent that each partner knows and trusts the other. So let's take time right now, the two of us, to get to know each other.

First of all, who is this guy Gittelson (that's me) and what makes him an authority on luck?

Fair question. Later on I'll go into more detail, drawing on incidents from my own life and experiences to illustrate each point I make. But for now, here's a quick rundown.

My parents were penniless immigrants who knew no English when they came to this country. I had to fight my way up from the word "go." But I gained confidence in myself early as I learned how to face problems and solve them. I soon realized that what had worked for me also had a chance of working for others—a fact that I immediately capitalized on and have continued to capitalize on.

At twenty-one, I read in the newspaper about a major problem confronting industries in New York State. I offered an *idea*. Again I sent a letter, which, believe it or not, most of the time gets read by the right people. I suggested that public hearings be held in the major cities in the state on the merits of a proposed law forbidding discrimination. This would put every official on record and thereby help to ensure ultimate passage of the law, which in fact happened. That idea not only sparked a job for myself, but led to a solution of the problem and eventually brought about a reform law that forbade discrimination in employment on the basis of race, creed, religion, or national origin. This law became the model for similar ones later passed in more than thirty states.

But the ripple effect didn't stop there. That job brought me into contact with a then relatively unknown artist, Arthur Szyk. Being a total innocent in business matters (like myself), he asked me as a favor to deal with a well-to-do patron, a Mr. Clarence, who wanted to buy a picture from him. The artist said to me, "You be my agent. Try to get five hundred dollars; settle for three-fifty. I'll go for a walk."

When Mr. Clarence arrived at three P.M. to look at the painting, I led him to believe the painting was already sold. "At least," I said, "someone said that he would call by three-thirty and give his decision. The price is fifteen hundred." Clarence looked annoyed and said it was too high for him—the most he would pay was a thousand. I said, "Let's wait until three-thirty. If he doesn't call, it's yours." We waited until three-thirty-one. I said, "It's yours." He was delighted, and the artist, when he saw the check, almost cried. He wrote out a check for one hundred dollars to me and said, "From now on, you're my agent." But again I didn't confine myself merely to business details—I made new contacts for him and brought him new *ideas* for future projects. That artist became rich and famous. I didn't do badly myself.

In my thirties I invested eight cents in an air-mail letter to the Chancellor of Germany. That letter contained a proposal relating to his country's upcoming diplomatic mission to the United States. I offered to act as their adviser on matters of public relations.

Crazy, you think? My PR firm had three employees and was three years old. My simple, commonsense approach to their problems won me the account against giants in the business. I proposed that I could help prevent errors rather than get headlines. (They'd had enough during the war.)

In time I built my public-relations firm into one of the world's largest, receiving sizable annual retainers per year for advising major corporations about what to do and what not to do. I sold out my interest in 1965. After twenty years of success and of traveling to Europe almost weekly, I felt it was time to change directions and become my own client.

I created a brand-new business of computerized astrology by taking an age-old field of lore that had been around for five thousand years and bringing it up-to-date with twentieth-century technology, even though at the outset I knew nothing about either astrology or computers. Up to that time a computer was used only for record keeping and calculations. This was the first time the computer output would be used as a consumer product. Later, after having the excitement of creating a new industry as well as a new product, I sold this company to a major conglomerate.

In my fifties I created a biorhythm business, based on data that had been discovered way back in 1890 but that nobody had known how to popularize. More than two million copies of my books on biorhythm have been sold, and I still write a syndicated biorhythm column for newspapers all over the world. I have become one of the leading authorities on the subject, by continuing my own research and by contacting everyone I can, all over the world who has any information. I have been around the world twice in search of new material.

And now, in my sixties, I've created a medical newsletter for the general public. At the same time, I'm writing this book and developing a device for improving the fuel efficiency of automobile engines, publishing a cookbook, and creating a company to develop and sell health products.

Okay, so much for me. Now let's take a look at you—a good, close look, because we're not going to deal in vague generalities. We want *facts.*

To get those facts, I'm going to ask you some questions. And I don't want pat answers off the top of your head. I want shrewd, insightful, tough-minded, carefully thought-out answers.

If it takes you all day to answer all or any of them adequately—fine. So much the better. That'll mean you're being forced to plow your way through a lot of clichés and platitudes and half-truths that may have been clogging your mind and fogging your outlook all these years. With such useless clutter disposed of, you can proceed to dig down deep for the truth.

All set, then? Good. Here goes.

1. What's Wrong with Your Life?

Presumably there must be *something* wrong with it. Otherwise if your life were perfect, why bother to read this book? Or is it a case of "Oh, well, my life's all right as far as it goes, but . . ."

But what? Spell it out. If something's wrong, now's the time to get it off your chest.

Maybe it's just a vague dissatisfaction. A feeling you're

not getting your share of all the good things life has to offer. Not enjoying each day to the fullest. Not achieving the things you hoped to achieve. Not forging ahead in business. Not having a job that's challenging enough. Not meeting the right people, not making enough friends. Whatever it is, put it down.

Or maybe your list of complaints includes some things that are definitely bad. Unpleasant circumstances that tend to spoil your daily existence. A bullying tyrant for a boss. A job that seems meaningless and takes up too much of your life. Debts hanging over your head. Depressing environment, ramshackle house, a slum neighborhood, a town devoid of stimulating opportunities or cultural attractions. Whatever's wrong—again, put it down.

Why are we starting out in this negative fashion, with this kind of gripe session? Because difficulties have to be pinpointed and brought out into the open before they can be corrected.

If your car's stalled, the mechanic must first locate the trouble before he can make repairs and get you back on the road. If you're not well, the doctor must diagnose the nature of your illness or the reason for your poor health before he can prescribe effective measures to get you in shape again.

By the same token, if you're not happy, then it's high time to ask yourself why—and do something about it.

So lay it on the line. Spell out exactly what's wrong with your present existence. Once you've done so, you will have taken the first step toward getting your life back on track.

2. What Do You Want Out of Life?

You wouldn't go into a store and expect the storekeeper to read your mind—at least not if you're sensible. You wouldn't just lay some money on the counter and wait for the clerk to put whatever he chooses into a bag, and still expect to walk out a satisfied customer.

First you have to *know* what you want and *tell* him what you've come to buy. If you've come for socks, you ask for socks. If it's a suit you want, you check out the stock in your size, select one you like, try it on in front of a mirror, and, if need be, get it altered for the best possible fit.

You watch how you spend your money and you know, more importantly, that you have only one life to live—only so many days to spend on this earth. If you must work for a living, as most of us do, then isn't it simple common sense to spend your time working at what *you* want?

Even Robin Hood could never have hit the bull's-eye if he hadn't had a visible target to shoot at. And you, too, need a target, a definite goal in life to aim for. To get anywhere in life, you must first decide *where* you want to go. You must pick a destination in order to set your course. Without a compass bearing to steer by, you'll veer in a different direction with every change of wind, drifting aimlessly on the sea of life.

So sharpen your pencil and start writing down, right now, exactly what you want out of this world. Is it more money? Improved social position? A better job? A more expensive home in an attractive community? Classier clothes? More success in your relations with the opposite sex? A greater measure of respect from the people around you? Maybe even some degree of fame? Don't be afraid of the word—come right out and say it: *I want to be famous.* Nothing wrong with that.

Okay, then, have you picked your goal in life? Do you know where you want to go?

Good. Now you've taken another important step toward changing your luck.

*   *   *

Let's pause now for two important tips.

Say you're a ditchdigger with a third-grade education, no business experience, and no marketable trade skills. But you've just written down that you want to become president of General Motors. Obviously there's not much point in choosing such an out-of-range target. If you write to the GM board of directors and apply for the position of president, I fear you've got a long wait for an answer.

Or let's say you're a middle-aged office clerk who's never been to college, but you'd like to become a brain surgeon. Then, my friend, I have some discouraging news for you. It's not likely to happen.

Mind you, I don't say it's *impossible*. Maybe you could take night courses to earn your college degree; then save up enough money and, if you can't get admitted to an American medical school, go somewhere abroad for your medical training; come back to this country for your internship and residency and eventually receive a license to practice medicine in the United States; later qualify as a surgeon and go on at long last to specialize in brain surgery.

It's a dazzling scenario, all right. Pure Horatio Alger, with a touch of science fiction. The only trouble is, the odds against your ever making it come true are about a million—more likely a hundred million—to one.

With those odds, why waste your time and money betting at all?

On the other hand, there's no reason why you can't hope to land a better office job than the one you now have, given the right effort, or earn fifty dollars more a week by moonlighting, or take an evening course in order to become a paramedic.

So my first tip is: *Choose a reasonable goal.*

My second tip simply carries that sensible thought just a little further.

Let's say you've been backpacking for days through

unfamiliar country. You come to a river. The place you're heading for lies on the other side. But the river's too deep for wading, you can't swim, and there's no bridge or ferry.

What do you do? Give up in despair and turn around and go home? Wait for a strong swimmer to come along who'll carry you over on his back? Plunge in and risk drowning?

Needless to say, none of these alternatives makes much sense. But just sighting your destination through binoculars and knowing that it lies on the other side of the river won't help much, either. It certainly won't get you across.

What should you do? Stand there and daydream helplessly? . . . Of course not.

How about going up a hill or climbing a tree or seeking some other high vantage point from which you can scout for a bridge or someone with a boat? Or how about exploring in both directions for a possible ford—either some shallower stretch of water or someplace with rocks sticking up on which you can scramble across safely?

Or, if you have an ax, you can fell a tree in such a way that it will fall across the river and thus provide you with a makeshift bridge. Or collect enough stout branches or pieces of driftwood to make a raft, or at least something to cling to that has enough buoyancy to keep you afloat while you paddle across.

In other words, it's not enough just to set your goal in life if that goal is realistically out of reach from your present position.

But don't stop there. Break the problem down into manageable steps by which you *can* hope to reach your goal. Don't just decide: My destination is that certain spot on the other side of this uncrossable river. Instead, start working out specific strategies to get across, as in the example above.

So right now review your goal in the light of common sense to make sure it's attainable. Then decide on your first move toward the attainment of that goal, for example:

- Look over the help-wanted ads in your local paper.
- Insert an ad of your own, to let prospective clients or employers know that you're available and what you have to offer.
- Check out training or self-improvement courses that may enhance your value as an employee.
- Join a club or take up some other leisure-time activity that will help you meet the kind of people you want to know.
- Take up a sport or get a book of exercises out of the library that will help to improve your physical condition and appearance, if that's part of your problem.
- Do something specific to make yourself liked or better liked by some person whose friendship you value or consider important.

All I ask is that this action or activity, whatever it may be, should add up to a first tentative move toward that goal in life you picked out earlier. (Remember the old proverb: The way to start walking is to get off your ass and move your legs.)

The minute you take that step, you will begin to change your luck. This I promise—provided, of course, you don't stop there.

3. What's Holding You Back?

Did ambition stir in you the moment you saw this book? Probably not. If you picked it up to glance through it or bought it at a store or ordered it by mail, I assume you were already aware of a certain lack of success in your life, of a need to improve your luck.

You must already have realized that you want something more out of life than you're getting—which in turn implies that something's been holding you back.

Am I correct? Do you have that feeling?

Okay, then, let's get down to brass tacks. What *has* been holding you back?

The present economic climate? Lack of education? Poor appearance? Inability to express yourself well in public? Burdensome responsibilities that tie you down to a daily grind at a no-future job rather than allow you to tackle some exciting but risky move toward a better tomorrow? The fact that you come from the wrong side of the tracks? Some social or physical stigma?

Good, glad to hear it, whatever your answer may be. The important thing is that now you've got this hidden obstacle out in the open. You know exactly what has to be changed or coped with. Doing so will be one of the first moves in your campaign for success.

What's more, you're doing the right thing by reading this book. Within these pages lies the help you've been seeking. I can confidently tell you, right off the bat, that none of these problems, whatever or however many they may be—repeat, *none* of these problems can hold you back from achieving success or improving your luck.

I give you that absolute assurance here and now.

At this moment I won't attempt to prove the truth of what I'm saying. For the time being, I ask you to take my word for it. Later on, I'll go into specifics and present you with all the evidence and case histories needed to convince you.

Meanwhile, rest assured that it's so, that none of those seeming obstacles can bar you from success and happiness. In fact they may actually provide you with valuable incentives toward achievement.

4. What Sort of Person Are You?

Take a good look in the mirror.

Why? Because you'll learn as we go along that all possibilities for success or failure exist *within yourself*. All capacity for change and growth exists within you and *only* you.

More immediately—in the beginning, at least—your ability to change the world outside you may be very slight or limited. What you *can* change is *yourself*.

Regardless of what you may think or have taken for granted, in the long run, no outside agency or set of circumstances can imprison you within a deprived, depressing, unsuccessful life-style. The truth is, the only villain who can do that to you is *you*.

By the same token, the only person who can upgrade your fortunes and win you a happier, more successful lifestyle is . . . *you*. It behooves you, therefore, to view yourself through the clearest, cleanest pair of spectacles you can lay hands on—or better yet, with no corrective lenses. The object is to see yourself, warts and all.

In the upcoming, ongoing battle for a happier, more successful life, your army is you. So, like any good general, you had better take a cold, hard look at your own strengths and weaknesses.

That famous British general, Wellington—a stiff-necked, hard-nosed disciplinarian, known as the Iron Duke—had no illusions about the army he led overseas to oppose the direst threat his country had yet faced. His soldiers were recruited from the foulest, most impoverished industrial slums; many were the sweepings of gutters and jails—"the scum of England," he called them. "They may not frighten the enemy, sir, but by Gad they frighten me." Yet with this so-called infamous army he crushed Napoleon at Waterloo and wrote finish to the career of the greatest conqueror Europe had seen up to that time.

In the skirmishes following the battles of Lexington and Concord, the Massachusetts Minute Men knew instinctively they were no match for the highly trained British redcoats on an open battlefield. So they sniped at them from behind stone walls and harried them mercilessly for mile after mile along their route of march. In doing so, they achieved one of the great guerrilla victories of history. They chased His Majesty's crack troops all the way back to Boston and kept them penned up there until the British finally quit in disgust and sailed off to New York.

To achieve what you want in life, you too need an effective strategy based on realistic self-knowledge. For example, which of these profiles best fits *your* case?

• You started off your career in fine style, but soon reached such a comfortable rut that you found it easier to relax and pull in your oars and simply drift along from week to week collecting an inadequate but dependable paycheck, with an eventual secure pension waiting after twenty years or so. (I hope inflation doesn't wipe your pension out.)

• You have always been too timid to try your luck in the rough-and-tumble of the public marketplace. Instead, you content yourself with daydreams that you never risk putting to the test.

• Having been burned on several occasions, you've given up trying and now spend your time sneering scornfully at real doers, while explaining to all and sundry how life's prizes are doled out on the basis of favoritism and connections, whereas a poor, honest, hardworking person like yourself has no chance whatever of scoring successfully on his or her own.

• You're planning to get going any day now. But meanwhile the time is not quite ripe for action, so it's only common sense to hold back and hoard your energies and

make all your preparations for that Big Moment—
which, of course, never actually comes.

• You'd like to strike out with some bold plan of action and
go into business for yourself, or upgrade your social
status, or convince the boss he should open a new
branch or department with you in charge, but so far
the breaks have gone steadily against you. You're
stuck with a big car-repair bill, and you can't afford a
decent new suit to help you make the grade, and your
wife's on tranquilizers to stave off a nervous breakdown, and next month your mother-in-law's coming
for an extended visit, and . . . well, you get the general
idea.

Do any of these thumbnail descriptions match your
personal situation? If not, write your own profile—and be
as brutally frank as you can. Then read it back as if you
were reading somebody else's case history.

You may be surprised at the extent to which it will
open your eyes. This single step alone may point the way
to a new and more effective life-strategy.

But don't stop there, *get down to details.*

Take a plain piece of paper and rule a vertical line
down the middle so as to divide the paper into two columns. In the left-hand column list all your personal *advantages,* and in the right-hand column all the *disadvantages*
under which you've been laboring.

As a guide and thought starter, and to make sure you
don't miss any important aspects or insights, I suggest you
use the following list of categories:

Health. What's the general state of your health? Do you
suffer from any serious physical handicaps or ailments that
might limit your activities or prevent you from undertaking
some specific, desirable project? Are you getting adequate

rest and relaxation? Have you the kind of vigorous, glow-ing health that tends to draw other people to you? Have you the stamina to engage in sustained, strenuous courses of action or to withstand periods of increased nervous ten-sion or emotional strain?

Appearance. Are you attractive or reasonably so? Is your outward image marred by any real or fancied blemishes that you fear may turn people off, such as acne or jug ears or a big nose? Are you short and looked down upon? Fat or skinny? Do you try to look younger or older than you really are? Have you an adequate wardrobe for the social and business demands facing you? Are you well groomed?

Education. Were you a high-school dropout? Did you ever get beyond elementary school? If you not only fin-ished high school but went on to college, did you graduate? Did you go on to graduate school and a higher degree? Or did you attend business school or trade school and learn a vocational skill? Or have you received on-the-job training that now fits you for a skilled trade? Have you acquired any special know-how or expertise from your family or en-vironment, such as the ability to speak a foreign language or to operate a particular kind of store or business?

Intelligence. Are you a quick learner? Do you have a good head for figures? Are you able to marshal facts as they apply to a particular situation and keep them clearly in mind? Can you pick other people's brains when necessary to compensate for your own deficiencies? Do you know how to go to the library and consult books, magazines, and other sources of information for whatever data you need? Do you read widely or not at all, aside from the daily news-paper? Are you capable of learning from the printed page, or do you have to have someone explain and show you?

Personality. Are you a shy, keep-to-yourself type or a good mixer? Are you mentally flexible, capable of turning your attention to new situations as they arise? Or are you a rigid, do-it-by-the-book, one-way-only type? Are you stubborn and persevering in carrying through a project, or are you easily discouraged? Are you capable of presenting your views clearly and forcefully? Or do you get tongue-tied and paralyzed when suddenly thrust into the spotlight? Have you the patience to cope with masses of tiresome detail? Or do you tend to rely on others for the detail work and excel only in carrying out the main thrust of a project? Are you energetic or lazy? Are you a hostile, hot-tempered type who tends to put people's backs up, or a friendly, easygoing person who generally manages to get along well with others?

Acquaintances. Do you have a wide circle of acquaintances whom you can consult or turn to in an emergency for specialized help or information? Or do you tend to confine yourself to a tight little group, speaking only to a few others with desks or workbenches next to yours, habitués of one favorite bar that you drop in at on your way home, the two or three neighbors directly across the street or whose yards adjoin yours? How easily do you make new friends? How often do you try?

Financial situation. Are you solvent? Have you any savings? Do you try to put something aside regularly in order to prepare for a rainy day or to accumulate capital? Are you hooked on charge accounts and credit cards? Do you purchase or invest wisely? Do you pick up your share of restaurant and bar checks? Do you overspend on hobbies and gifts? On clothes? On vacations? Do you understand the difference between stinginess and selfishness, and genuine financial prudence? What is the extent of your present indebtedness, and in what major categories?

Background. Can your family help you, or do they need your financial help? Have you deep roots in the community, or did you recently move from some other part of the country? Do you feel yourself to be strictly white-collar or blue-collar, or can you mingle comfortably with any social stratum? Do you feel comfortable at a formal dinner? Can you hold up your end of the conversation with people from other walks of life or only with people who share your own life-style and interests? How would you describe your accustomed life-style?

Environment. Do you live in the country, a suburb or city or a ghetto? Is this where you *prefer* to live? Are you situated within reach of good cultural, educational, and business facilities? Or is it a location you'd be more inclined to call "the boondocks" or a "cultural desert"?

If you've done as I suggested, and used the above list of categories as a source of pluses and minuses, by now you may well have a long list of *disadvantages.* Is that indeed your case? Nothing but one grim handicap after another?

Don't let it worry you for a minute. You've just passed the acid test to qualify as a preferred reader of this book.

I guarantee that *not one* of those disadvantages need stand in the way of your success. Regardless of how many handicaps you may suffer from, none of them can prevent you from improving your situation in life.

What's more, I'd be willing to bet that you also discovered you had a good many more advantages than you previously realized. Which brings up the question, How fully are you capitalizing on those advantages?

In any case, once you've taken that good, hard look at yourself and gone through the whole quiz that I've outlined in this chapter, you probably know yourself just a little bit better than you did before—at least well enough to plan a new and more successful strategy in life. Which leads us to the last two questions:

5. What Have You Done So Far?

Before reading this book, did you act to improve your lot in life? If your efforts didn't work, why not? What caused them to fizzle?

6. What Are You Doing Now?

Nothing, you say? At any rate nothing more successful than your previous abortive attempts?

Then it's high time we got on to the next chapter.

2

What Is Luck?

*W*ebster's New Collegiate Dictionary defines luck as "a force that brings good fortune or adversity; the events or circumstances that operate for or against an individual."

I like that definition because it's so clear and to the point. More important to us here, it may help you understand at the very outset what this book is all about. The key words are "force" and "events or circumstances."

Why? Because these are what cause good things to happen.

Maybe you weren't aware of that before. If you're like most people, you probably never realized that good fortune is *caused*. And since it's caused, *anyone* can study and master this cause-and-effect process, and thus bring about good fortune for himself or herself.

Yes, that's right. *You, too, can make your own good luck happen.*

I can imagine your reaction to this statement. I can almost see you cocking a skeptical eyebrow. But just hang in there and trust me for a moment.

Here are four examples that I'd like you to study and analyze:

1. An elderly barber named Sal Iovagna recently won $100,000 in a state-run lottery—enough to support him and his wife in comparative luxury for the rest of their lives.

2. John Dorfman is one of five young executives employed in a steel company based in Akron, Ohio. Recently he was named manager of a newly opened branch office in Phoenix, Arizona—whereupon the other four young executives muttered enviously under their breath, *"That lucky dog."*

3. A little boy named Morgan Rowe suddenly saw his family faced with staggering bills and wanted to do his bit to help pay them off. He turned up some of the needed money—just by looking along the road.

4. An unskilled blue-collar worker named Steve Jaworski was recently laid off along with half a dozen of his fellow workers on a county-road maintenance crew. They lost their jobs during a round of political budget pruning and belt tightening. The other six have gone on welfare and are looking, not very hopefully, for new jobs. Unlike them, Steve is now earning twice as much money as he was before, running his own paving and patching service.

Each of these people was "lucky" in his own way. But, on closer examination, some important differences instantly come to light.

For instance, when Sal Iovagna won that lottery, he beat out odds of something like half a million to one. John Dorfman and little Morgan Rowe, on the other hand, were bucking no odds at all, as I shall show you later. For all practical purposes, each was onto a sure thing. Steve Jaworski's situation is a little harder to assess statistically, but at worst he was probably facing odds of no more than two or three to one.

What odds would *you* prefer to face in your search for success? Sky-high, long-shot odds of half a million or a million to one or something much closer to even Steven?

Foolish question, isn't it? Yet, believe it or not, most people (if they lift a finger at all to improve their luck) are content to bet against the house by relying on such pathetic strategies as playing the numbers, attending bingo nights, or buying weekly lottery tickets. Buoyed on such flimsy life preservers of hope, they go on wistfully daydreaming, month after month and year after year, that someday their ship will come in.

If those are the odds you're trying to beat—odds of hundreds of thousands to one—you've come to the wrong expert. Try the nearest witch doctor or Gypsy wise woman.

"Luck" of this kind is hardly classifiable as luck at all. So many possible different outcomes can result from the spin of a wheel or a drawing from a hopper, depending on a near infinity of intangible influences, that what happens becomes a "random event," subject only to "blind chance." That's why gambling games are often called—in fact, in some jurisdictions legally *must* be called —"games of chance."

Needless to say, I didn't write this book to teach you how to gamble. I wrote it to teach you how to manipulate the odds so as to *ensure* that you will enjoy at least the more modest kind of luck achieved by John Dorfman and Morgan Rowe and Steve Jaworski. More modest, yes, but in the long run far more satisfying and permanent—and more likely. Study after study proves that compulsive gamblers who insist on worshiping at the shrine of the blind goddess of chance invariably wind up broke.

John Dorfman, Morgan Rowe, and Steve Jaworski, on

the other hand, can repeat their kind of lucky feats *more or less at will.* Thus all three can confidently look forward to building themselves solid, successful careers.

To see why, let's take another, closer look at those same four cases.

Aside from shelling out fifty cents to buy that lottery ticket at the corner newsstand, Sal Iovagna did nothing but wait for the drawing to take place. Obviously there was nothing more he *could* do—no way in which he could influence the outcome.

Not so John Dorfman. John, on his own time and initiative, ran a series of computer studies showing that the Phoenix area was expanding faster than anyplace else in the country as a market for his company's products, with a growth rate of over 300 percent in the last four years. Moreover, he analyzed that particular area to determine, for example, its likely future trends as to population growth, new construction, specific types of items most frequently ordered, available financing, and present shipping versus warehousing costs.

With this kind of hard-nosed market data, he was able to convince his boss, and ultimately the company's top brass, that opening a new branch in Phoenix was likely to be a highly profitable move. Naturally, by the time they decided to make that move Dorfman had already established himself as the obvious and logical man to head up the new operation.

He didn't merely *wait* and *hope* that, if and when the company ever *should* open a new branch office in Phoenix, his superiors *might* choose him from among five equally eager young executives to manage it—not to mention various other, in some instances more senior, candidates long waiting their turn for promotion. John Dorfman *made his own luck.*

Young Morgan Rowe didn't just walk along the side of the road looking for stray coins or lost valuables—though possibly he discovered a few from time to time. What he picked up were redeemable pop bottles and recyclable aluminum cans. He didn't rely on blind chance. He knew, as everyone else knows, that these discards litter many of our streets and roads. Unlike most people, Morgan was willing to expend the time and effort to pick up such "worthless" trash and cash in on it.

Steve Jaworski, in the course of maintaining county roads, had noticed that a lot of householders had sidewalks and driveways in need of slight repairs. Those cracks or holes weren't bad enough to justify the expense of laying a whole new pavement or drive; they were, however, the kind of nuisance chore that most people tend to keep putting off and putting off, simply because they require a certain amount of forethought, preliminary preparation and expense, and a modicum of physical effort.

Steve had moonlighted in his spare time and on weekends, performing such mending jobs, and he knew the business was there. A steady trickle of calls kept coming in from two ads placed in local community newspapers and from householders who had seen him doing such work for their neighbors. True, he had no advance assurance that the volume of work available would sustain a full-time job. Even so, the extra income was sure to be a big help in supporting his family during the layoff period.

As things turned out, his emergency enterprise not only *did* become a full-time job; Steve is now investing in heavy equipment and bidding on full-scale jobs as paving contractor.

By now the difference between the lottery winner and the other three cases should be even more evident. The lottery winner did *nothing but wait and hope.* The other three *worked actively* to bring about their good luck.

Let me pause for a moment to ask you something personal. It's really just a slight rephrasing of something I asked you at the close of the previous chapter.

Question: What have you done recently (if anything) to bring about any changes in your own life? For example:

- Have you tried putting out just a little bit more effort than your job officially calls for?
- Have you tried to show your spouse or lover, by any little extra attentions, how much affection and appreciation you feel for him/her?
- Have you tried in any way, however trivial, to win a new friend, or make a new acquaintance, or make yourself a bit more attractive to the opposite sex?
- Have you tried to expand your mental horizons in any way, by, say, reading or museum-going, before you got hold of this book?
- Have you done anything at all recently to convince your boss that you deserve advancement?
- If any aspect of your home life, neighborhood environment, or work routine has become a depressing pain in the neck, have you tried, just *tried*—however trivially or ineffectively—to improve it for the better?
- If your job is truly a dead end or just plain intolerable, have you done anything at all to look for some other sort of gainful employment or enterprise—even if it was only to turn to the help-wanted or business-opportunities section of your local newspaper or to consult a friend for ideas? Or have you just *daydreamed* about "getting a lucky break"?

Let's go back once more to those four examples we were discussing. There's still another factor at work in these cases, which may not have occurred to you yet may be the most important factor of all.

Our barber friend, Sal Iovagna, from all indications, had led a fairly happy life, even if only in modest circumstances. He was resigned to the prospect of retiring one of these days on Social Security plus his lifetime savings of nearly $13,000, which, together with ownership of his present house, would have been enough to resettle him and his wife in a Florida retirement community, should they choose to move there, or to live out the rest of their days in relative comfort, close to their married children.

His weekly purchase of a lottery ticket, up to the moment of his big win, was no more than a small self-indulgence—a weekly prayer and a hope that might or might not pay off. The fact that it did happen to pay off was due to nothing more than *blind chance*.

John Dorfman's case is quite different. John is an individual burning with ambition. Although his whole outlook is that of an "organization man," and although he'll probably spend his entire life as a corporation employee rather than operate a business of his own, nevertheless he's impelled by a strong, *competitive upward drive* that will almost certainly carry him to the top echelon of corporate command. His smoothly plotted and carried-out campaign to become manager of a new branch office is merely one step along the way.

Morgan Rowe is only *ten years old,* yet this amazing little boy is every bit as determined to succeed as John Dorfman. At the age of six Morgan lost one arm in a tractor accident and still has only limited use of the other. The ambulance bill alone came to $455. The six-year-old accident victim vowed matter-of-factly, "Mother, I'll pay it."

He not only did pay it, but went on doggedly grinding away at his family's financial burden. Reynolds Aluminum learned what Morgan was doing and put him in touch with the Bear Archery Company, of Gainesville, which manufactures aluminum arrows. The company said it would give its spare metal to Morgan's scrap drive. Morgan recently presented a check of $17,713 to the South Georgia Medical Center, the final installment of his $30,000 medical bill.

Some people would classify this as "luck"—and they'd be right. It's luck that Morgan *made himself.*

Steve Jaworski was a high-school dropout, seemingly limited to a depressing future of unskilled manual labor. Nevertheless, following his marriage and especially after the birth of his first child four years ago, Steve grew more and more determined to start a business of his own in which his possible earnings would be limited only by his own efforts.

The notion of patching drives and sidewalks didn't come to him just by chance, like a bolt out of the blue. Long before getting laid off and taking the plunge into self-employment, he had already tried moonlighting at such chores as handyman, tree pruning, house painting, and fence building. Pavement mending was only one of a whole series of ideas for self-employment that Steve had considered and talked over with his wife, who now acts as his bookkeeper and order taker. He settled on this particular work only after trial moonlighting attempts convinced him that a greater market existed for this particular service than for any of the others he was prepared to offer.

By now it should be clear that our three cases of "modest success" share two other important qualities in common.

First, all three of these individuals were *strongly motivated* to succeed.

Second, all of them were aiming at *definite goals.*

They knew what they wanted, and they wanted it so badly that they could almost taste it.

Wanting something intensely is the motivating power that produces good luck. It's the steam that makes your personal steam engine of success go.

There's an old story about how James Watt, the Scottish inventor who helped to perfect the steam engine, got his first ideas on the subject by watching his mother's kettle on the stove. No doubt he saw the lid start to dance up and down as the boiling water became steam. But he also realized that the lid would never be forced off as long as most of the steam could escape harmlessly through the spout.

These and other observations pointed clearly to the fact that steam could be used as a driving force—but only if it were concentrated and directed so as to push against a piston and thus perform useful work. Otherwise it would simply dissipate in the air.

By the same token, if you want something intensely enough to go after it, that driving urge can propel you successfully to your goal. But you must *harness* that power into effective *action*—which takes planning, determination, and perseverance. Otherwise it leaks away uselessly in the form of bar-stool hot air and porch-swing musings.

Remember, the stuff of daydreams is the same as the stuff of success. But in the latter case it's been shaped into a successful end product. It's like a block of marble, which is just a hunk of stone until the sculptor makes it into a beautiful statue. The statue was there in essence all the time—it took the sculptor's vision and energy and know-how to bring it out into the open.

Your ambitions and desires, too, are a vision that can be turned into reality. This book will teach you the know-how. But only *you* can provide the *energy*.

So far we've been talking mostly about luck versus blind chance.

Blind chance is how one person out of hundreds of thousands of other people, or even millions of others, happens to win a fortune in a lottery or stumble on a lost wallet stuffed with cash. No sensible person bases his future hopes on such a one-in-a-million occurrence. If he does, he's asking for, and indeed ensuring, ultimate disappointment.

Do you think Irving Berlin, who started his career in this country as a penniless, fatherless Russian immigrant boy, just happened to become America's most popular songwriter by blind chance?

Do you think Al Capp, wooden-legged creator of the *Li'l Abner* comic strip, just happened to become a successful cartoonist by blind chance?

Do you think George Washington Carver, a black man born a slave, just happened to become a successful scientist and inventor by blind chance?

You don't even need to know the details of these people's lives to recognize at once how ridiculous the question is. Common sense alone tells us that each one *made his own luck.*

But now let's go back and look at that definition of luck: "a force that brings good fortune or adversity; the events or circumstances that operate for or against an individual."

Notice particularly the phrases "good fortune or adversity" and "operate for or against."

In other words, luck can be good or bad, as everyone knows. What you may never have realized is that bad luck or failure can be self-made just as readily as good luck or success.

No need to dwell on this thought. It's far better to fill your mind with positive thoughts than with negative ones.

All the same, it never hurts to remember that actions do tend to cause results. Therefore, our own actions may either sour our luck or improve it. The choice is up to us. If you fail, you have learned something and you can now start again, wiser.

For example, does common sense tell you that antagonizing people, squandering your money foolishly, wasting opportunities, allowing yourself to get out of shape physically, blaming others when something goes wrong, or closing your mind to new information will help to improve your chances of a successful career?

Of course not. Foolish question, you say. Yet the implications are far reaching and may not have occurred to you.

Let me sum it up this way: All actions tend to produce results, good or bad. *No* action tends to produce *no* result.

But hold it. Did you notice?

With those alternatives, you've just used up all your options. In other words:

1. You can indulge in the kind of negative, antagonistic, self-defeating behavior that produces failure.

2. You can sit back and do nothing—in which case your situation may not get any worse, but it's not likely to get any better, either.

3. Or you can adopt the kind of positive, productive, self-helping behavior that makes for success.

The fact is that every day, at all times, willy-nilly, like it or not, you're engaging in one of those three types of behavior. You can't help it. You can't hold back the hands of the clock or stop the world because you want to get off. For better or worse, every hour of every day, you're writing your own destiny, dictating the prophecy in your own fortune cookie.

The forecast can be depressing or merely boring or positively great. The choice is up to you.

The one thing you *can't* do is wish yourself into a state of suspended animation, like a bear hibernating for the winter. Fortunately or unfortunately, hibernation is not a feature of human life. With each new day we go on existing, functioning, and playing out our chosen roles until we finally, in Shakespeare's immortal words, shuffle off this mortal coil.

Which role have you chosen for *your*self?

Success? Failure? A continued average, humdrum, aimless, grumbling, run-of-the-mill existence as just another member of the common herd, with no more success or friends or love or money or happiness than you have right now?

I repeat: The choice is yours; the future is up to you—because *luck* is what *you* make it.

HOMEWORK

Turn back to page 28, where I listed the three courses that will tend to shape your life. In describing them, I spoke of negative, antagonistic, self-defeating behavior, sitting back and doing nothing, and positive, productive, self-helping behavior.

Notice especially that I used the word "behavior." There was a reason for doing so, an important reason.

Actions may be one of a kind—something we perform just once or rarely, on some particular occasion or at certain times. When we tend to *repeat* those actions regularly, over and over, day after day, they become *behavior*.

The fact is, most of us are creatures of habit. As we grow up we learn to behave in a certain way and tend to go on behaving that same way unless and until we're confronted by some shattering, overwhelming experience, such as Paul's vision on the road to Tarsus, which converted him to Christianity. Or the experience can be wartime combat, a shocking accident, a narrow escape from death by heart attack, or perhaps contact with some inspiring teacher or strong personality who changes one's whole outlook on life.

If you feel yourself to be a failure, or at least not as successful as you would like to be, I hope I have convinced you by now that this is due to your own pattern of behavior.

Obviously, then, to improve your luck and become more successful, you must *change* your ingrained, customary behavior. This book will teach you a new pattern of behavior, which I guarantee can help to upgrade your present level of success and happiness.

But you don't need to wait till you get to the last chapter of the book. You can start right now, today—just in a small way, perhaps—to change your life.

Here's how: Think over your typical daily, weekly routine. Better yet, get pencil and paper and jot it all down in black and white, as an aid to focusing your thoughts.

From among your regular activities try to pick out *just one* that seems to you particularly wasteful, harmful, or at least nonproductive. Then make up your mind to change it for the better, *starting now.*

For example, maybe you spend an hour a day on a commuter train or bus, just staring out the window or woolgathering. Why not spend that time reading some book or magazine that will increase your present store of useful information?

Or maybe you drive to work listening to music on your car tape deck. Instead, why not invest in some instructional tapes and spend at least part of that daily driving time improving your educational level, perhaps by learning a foreign language?

Or maybe you have a habit of dropping into a bar on the way home for two or three rounds of drinks with your buddies, accompanied by a more or less standard vein of barroom conversation in which you air your gripes against the world, gossip about the various attractive people you'd like to have sex with, or explain how you'd steer the home team to a world championship if the owner just had brains enough to hire you instead of that present idiot manager.

From now on, why not cut out one drink, get home earlier, and invest the time and money thus saved in a program of personal improvement? Or, if you haven't the willpower to cut down on the number of drinks, try picking your barroom buddies' brains for a change, and learn some new, useful items of expertise.

If your job involves dealing with the public, do you regularly greet people with a scowl or answer questions in surly monosyllables, thereby making it about as easy to get information out of you as it is to pull teeth? Or do you ease the daily emotional tension by venting your bad temper on anyone who dares to overstep what you consider the permissible bounds of customer behavior?

Beginning now, why not decide to smile (at least part of the time) and be extra helpful to some customer you might normally brush off? Or, if you're confronted by someone unpleasant, instead of snapping back, try responding with pleasant, even-tempered politeness, thereby showing him or her that your good nature is not vulnerable to ill-tempered boors. (Maybe you'll even convert *him* to more pleasant manners.)

None of these behavior changes are earth shaking, perhaps, but it's in small ways like these that you can start *today* to *change your life*.

3

You've Got It

(Otherwise Known As
"Eliminate the Negative")

*E*ver shoot craps? If so, you know it's a game in which you can lose a bundle fast when the dice go against you.

But suppose I were to show you a gambling game that you *can't lose.* Would you be interested in playing it? . . . Foolish question, huh? Who wouldn't?

Well, that's the kind of game I propose to teach you in this book. It's a real-life game in which the stakes are a better job, more money in the bank, more happiness, more whatever-you-want-out-of-life. And you can't lose.

All it takes is the will and energy to play. The stakes are out there on the board, just waiting to be raked in. And, I repeat, you can't lose.

Who could resist such a game? Millions of people do. And presumably, until now, you've been one of them—a nonplayer—otherwise you wouldn't be reading this book.

Well, if that's the case, let's not let another day go by with you missing out on your share of the loot. Let's start you playing in there as fast as possible.

Let's demonstrate. Take a coin, say an ordinary Lincoln penny. The play consists of tossing the coin to see how it lands. Obviously it can fall only in either of two ways—heads or tails, right? So pick whichever side you prefer.

Heads, you say? Okay, fine. Let heads stand for whatever you're after in life—more money, a better job, a happier environment, you name it.

Now toss the coin. . . .

It landed heads? That's terrific. You're lucky right off the bat. On your very first try you've won what you wanted.

But suppose it *didn't* land heads up. Say it turned up tails. No problem—because here's the wonderful thing about this game I'm teaching you: Even though the coin didn't land the way you wanted, that doesn't diminish your chances of success.

There's no penalty at all when the coin doesn't land right. You can keep on tossing, again and again, as often as you like, until it does land right.

In other words, *you can't lose.*

It may take you just one more throw or five or ten more. It doesn't matter how many because, sooner or later, the coin is bound to land heads up. And when it does, you win.

How's that for a game, my friend? Believe me, that's exactly how the game of success is played in real life.

All it takes is the willingness to throw the dice—meaning the gumption and energy to get up off the seat of your pants and *try.* If you *keep* trying, you're a certain winner. Just keep on rolling the dice and *you can make your own luck.*

In the old days, when pupils were still taught reading and history in school, sooner or later almost every kid would run across the story of Robert Bruce and the spider.

Bruce was king of Scotland. Six times his army had been beaten by the English. With his forces shattered,

Bruce was finally driven to take shelter in a tiny shed. As he lay there, feeling sorry for himself, he watched the spider spinning its web. Six times the tiny creature tried to run a strand from one beam to another. Each time it fell short. But it kept trying, and on the seventh try it succeeded.

Inspired and shamed into action by the spider, Bruce gathered his army together for another try. This time his kilted warriors smashed the English invaders at Bannockburn and won their country's independence.

Theodor S. Geisel—better known under his pen name of Dr. Seuss—tells how his first children's book, *And to Think That I Saw It on Mulberry Street,* was rejected twenty-three times.

As he was lugging the manuscript down the street, about ready to give up, he ran into an old college friend. His friend, as it turned out, had become an editor of children's books. He invited Geisel to step into his office and show him the manuscript. The rest, as they say, is history. Dr. Seuss is now the world's most popular children's author; his books have sold millions of copies and been animated for television, and earned him a fortune.

At this point I can almost hear you saying, "But I don't have an old college chum who can give me a hand when I need it."

Makes no difference.

The point is, both Robert Bruce and Ted Geisel were *doers* and *triers* and *perseverers.* If they hadn't succeeded one way, you can bet your bottom dollar they would have succeeded another way. Bruce could have gone to lick his wounds after five defeats; Geisel could have given up after he was turned down twenty times. Instead of waiting for luck, they went out and *made* it.

You, too, along with every other human being, have this precious power within you. And there's nothing extraordinary about it.

By acting, you make things happen. And with a little practice and planning, you can make them happen your way.

I wish I could see you face to face, so I could tell you this in person and convince you of just how fervently I believe and *know* that this is true.

Never mind. In his recent book, *My Young Years,* that great piano virtuoso Arthur Rubinstein says it far better than I can. So let me quote him.

In response to someone who says, "You are indeed a lucky man," Rubinstein replies: "Yes, I am very lucky, but I have a little theory about this. I have noticed through experience and observation that providence, nature, God, or what I would call the power of creation seems to favor human beings who *accept and love life unconditionally,* and I am certainly one who does with all my heart. So I have discovered as a result of what I can only call miracles that whenever my inner self desires something subconsciously, life will somehow grant it to me."

Although Rubinstein uses the word "miracles," you'll notice he also points out that this happens automatically as a natural law of life. In other words, you can have anything you want if you want it badly enough to go after it.

Call this a miracle, call it driving instinct, call it the power of luck or whatever you like. The point is that you, as a living organism, already have this power of luck. And every day you go on living *proves* how lucky you are.

You doubt my word? Let me cite a few statistics.

You were born, right? Yet only one sperm in 250 million penetrates the egg. And even so, not every embryo makes it to birth.

Furthermore, to reach your present age, you had to survive all the potential diseases and accidents of infancy and childhood, not to mention the hazards of war, floods, tornadoes, and the risk of getting run down by drunken drivers. Yet despite all these odds, here you are.

Don't tell me you're not lucky. And you've now acquired another big advantage: You're reading this book.

But let's look a little closer. Presumably you're eating more or less regularly. You have a roof over your head, clothes on your back. You've learned to read, to function safely and successfully from day to day.

That means you've already learned how to influence circumstances, how to interact with others in a way to fulfill your basic needs, how to take advantage to some degree of whatever breaks have come your way so far. Basically, then, you're *already* on the road to success. These are the same sorts of things you have to do in order to *make your own luck*.

All I'm going to do is teach you the knack of doing them more often, more consciously, more effectively. What do I mean by "influence circumstances" and "interact with others"?

A baby in the crib is wet or hungry. He cries loudly. His mother comes to feed him or change his diaper, after which he drifts peacefully off to sleep. If not, she rocks him in her arms until he dozes off. Once this has happened a few times, the baby learns that crying brings attention. Thereafter, whenever he wants something, he cries.

Already the infant has learned to control the world around him—in effect, to make his own luck.

A schoolboy wants to go to the movies on a school night. But his father asks sternly, "Is your homework done?" Squirming, the boy admits that it isn't, so his request is refused.

Thereafter, on any night he wants to go out, he makes sure his homework gets done early. Result: His luck improves; he gets the hoped-for permission.

A high-school girl working as a carhop has a crush on

a certain boy. One night she sees his car enter the drive-in. It's not her turn to wait on that particular car, but she makes a quick deal with one of the other carhops in order to do so. Result: She gets a chance to talk and flirt with the boy of her dreams, and they wind up making a date. By controlling circumstances, then, she has acquired the boyfriend she hoped for.

Examples like these are so commonplace that we tend to overlook them or take them for granted. They're so much a part of our day-to-day living that we may forget that exactly the same techniques apply in achieving adult success.

Take a mail-room boy who hopes someday to be promoted to his company's sales staff. At lunchtime, in the plant cafeteria, he makes it a point to sit down and chat with any members of the sales department he spots—occasionally including even the sales manager himself. This gives him a chance to establish his image as an eager-beaver type who's thoroughly knowledgeable about the company's products and conversant with practical selling problems.

Result: When an opening in the sales department occurs, he'll be one of the first to know about it; what's more, he'll already have done much of the spadework needed to land the job.

In effect, both the carhop and the mail-room boy are using exactly the same ploy, or success technique, whichever you prefer to call it. Both are manipulating circumstances in order to bring about contacts that will lead to a desired goal.

And the same old homespun, time-tested techniques apply to handling *people*.

A pretty little girl throws her arms around her visiting grandpa's neck and plants a big kiss on his cheek. The beaming grandparent promptly slips her fifty cents. On seeing this, a cynical observer might accuse the little girl of manipulating Grandpa for money.

Well, maybe so. On the other hand, if she truly loves her grandpa, and if expressing her affection in the form of a hug and kiss helps to make them both happy, what's wrong with that?

Not infrequently, a husband has been known to bring home candy or flowers, or compliment the wife on her cooking, or whisper sweet nothings in her ear, on nights when he particularly wants to make love. Call it manipulating the love relationship if you like. Or just say the husband is acting in a way that experience has shown is likely to get results.

A clothing salesman may enthusiastically compliment a customer on the way he looks when he tries on an expensive suit. Why? Because the salesman knows from experience that such compliments may help to resolve the customer's secret doubts over whether or not he's making the right choice, and thus help him make up his mind to buy the suit.

Do you know what I've just been doing? I've been showing you how people *make their own luck*.

These examples are too simple, you say?

Nonsense. That's what luck is all about. That's all it amounts to—namely, doing something to bring about a desired result rather than just waiting and hoping for that result to happen by chance or of its own accord.

Take the biggest, cleverest, shrewdest, most successful business deal ever consummated, and you'll find it boils down to exactly the same elements. The businessman who negotiated the deal wanted something for himself, and, having checked out the situation beforehand, he knew that the other party was also willing to talk turkey if supplied with whatever *he* wanted. Tit for tat. So they got together, worked out terms, and closed the deal.

In short, the businessman knew how to press the right buttons to get the right result.

Recently the Pan Am skyscraper in New York City was sold for something like half a billion dollars. The seller got the money *he* wanted; the buyer got the real estate investment *he* wanted. Both were happy.

Now, the promoter who brought the two parties together might well be called *lucky*. And certainly half a billion dollars is a fabulous sum of money. Yet aside from the sheer scale of the deal, there's basically no difference between the sale of the Pan Am Building and the example of that little girl who kissed her grandpa and got fifty cents.

In both cases a mutually beneficial arrangement was effected by virtue of someone doing the right thing at the right time.

Let's pause to examine that phrase "doing the right thing at the right time," or, as the same concept is often expressed in slightly different words, "being in the right place at the right time."

To many people this concept is laden with mystery. They think it involves some deep, dark secret known only to those lucky few who become millionaire business tycoons.

Again, nonsense. It means exactly what it says—no more, no less.

Say you have to be to work at eight o'clock in the morning and you start out by train or bus or car soon enough to arrive and punch in on schedule. That's one example of being in the right place at the right time—and thereby accomplishing the valuable goal of hanging on to your present income-producing employment.

No, I'm not trying to be funny. I mean it.

Or say you need a job. You look in the help-wanted section of the newspaper and see three openings that seem as if they might be suited to your capabilities. You call two of the companies that advertised and get nowhere; maybe those jobs have already been filled. But the third place gives you an appointment for an interview.

You show up, have the interview, and make a good impression. The personnel manager sees that you're exactly the kind of qualified worker he's looking for, so he hires you on the spot. Bingo—you're in.

Would you call that being in the right place at the right time? . . . Of course.

And would you also call it luck? . . . Why not?

The point is, there is nothing mysterious about it. You needed a job, so you took perfectly ordinary, obvious, commonsense steps to find one. As a result, you wound up being in the right place at the right time.

And it didn't just happen by accident.

Or take another simple example. If you're a male, very likely at some time in your life you've found yourself in a parked car with a girl and kissed her—which certainly constitutes being in the right place at the right time.

Nothing very mysterious about that, surely. When it happened, did you consider yourself lucky? Probably so, and with good reason—it was highly enjoyable. I'll go along with that. The prettier the girl, the luckier you were.

The point is, however thrilling or wonderful an experience it may have seemed at the time, the whole thing was quite fundamental to human nature—even commonplace. You were simply acting on an impulse common to millions and millions of other young men like yourself since time immemorial. You met a girl who attracted you, you invited her out on a date, you steered her to a suitably romantic and secluded spot, and—it happened.

Sure, maybe it involved a little planning or persuasion

or timing on your part—not to mention keeping an eye out for the right girl to ask out. But it took no heaven-sent magical charm or anything else out of the ordinary. Basically, *you made your own luck.*

You didn't require any elaborate college course of instruction or learned academic treatise on how to kiss a girl; nor did you need a complicated campaign strategy worked out by a staff of secretaries and assistants. You simply knew what you wanted and did what came naturally to accomplish it.

Now do you understand what I mean by "luck?" And why I say that you, too, can be lucky?

Perhaps what tends to throw most people is the seemingly giant step of carrying over these simple, basic life experiences into the field of business or their career. "Oh, my gosh," they think, "surely it can't be that simple." But believe me, it is. Precisely the same principles work in both areas.

As Americans we traditionally feel ourselves to be luckier than most people in other parts of the world. And well we may. In this country we enjoy liberty, security, bountiful agricultural output, advanced technology, good medical services, one of the world's highest standards of living—in short, a relative abundance of everything that makes life worth living. People in every part of the globe tend to envy our happy situation. They feel instinctively that the United States is "where it's at."

What we ourselves often tend to forget is that all this didn't come about just by chance or because some good fairy touched this country with her magic wand. It happened because certain gutsy people in the Old World grew dissatisfied with their lot and decided to do something about it; they risked life and limb to cross the ocean in fragile wooden sailing ships in order to carve new homes for their families out of a hostile wilderness; or, later on, they came over packed in steerage like cattle and worked and sweated in unfriendly cities in order to lift themselves out of the slums by their bootstraps and achieve a better way of life for their children.

This is *luck?* . . . You're damned right. That's *exactly* what luck is. It's *sweat* and *hard work* and *sacrifice* and *planning ahead* and *taking calculated risks* in order to improve your future.

In short, when your present lot in life is not to your liking, good luck consists of doing something about it.

Every living organism has certain needs, and is equipped by nature with the means to satisfy those needs in order to go on existing. You as a living organism are equipped by nature to satisfy your needs. In other words, nature has equipped you with all that it takes to make your own luck.

Therefore, if you're not as lucky as you'd like to be, it must be because you're *not doing anything about it.*

Perhaps that statement tends to put your back up. "Like hell it's my fault," you retort. "Look at all the obstacles and handicaps I have to contend with."

Well, okay—let's look at them. In Chapter 1 I asked you to list all the disadvantages that you feel have been holding you back from success. Take that list out again now and read them off. Presumably they include one or more of the following:

- I'm physically handicapped.
- I'm unattractive because of certain blemishes or a lack of desirable physical attributes.
- I don't have enough education.
- I come from the wrong side of the tracks and therefore lack poise and finesse.
- I haven't enough money to afford the right kind of clothes and grooming to create a good impression.

- I'm handicapped by shyness or other personality traits.
- I lack the kind of pull or influence needed to get ahead.
- I'm a member of a disadvantaged minority group with no possible chance to break out of the ghetto or overcome the prejudices confronting me.
- It's too late for me because I'm too old.
- I'm already a failure.

No doubt I've missed some points—people always demonstrate inventive genius when it comes to making excuses for themselves. But I think the above list is complete enough to make my point.

And just what *is* my point? It's that *none* of these disadvantages has the slightest chance of blocking your way to success—that is, not if you *want* to succeed badly enough. In fact they may even provide you with valuable incentives to get up on your hind legs and climb out of your present rut.

Let me offer a few case histories to prove my statement.

You're unattractive, you say—you lack the physical attributes for success. Whatever gave you that notion? Some people might call Dudley Moore very short, but that hasn't prevented him from becoming a national sex symbol, following his big success in the hit movie *"10."*

Another shorty, Alan Ladd, became one of Hollywood's most sought-after leading men, despite the fact that his female co-stars often had to stand in holes or else he had to mount a box during their on-camera embraces. Barbra Streisand refused to have her nose bobbed, yet went on to become one of the screen's top glamour goddesses—not merely as a singer but in romantic heart-throb roles such as Robert Redford's sweetheart in *The Way We Were.*

Humphrey Bogart, Jean-Paul Belmondo, and Charles Bronson would all be considered homely, even ugly, by ordinary standards, yet each became a Great Lover in the movies. British actor Michael Rennie had a face scarred by acne, which he never troubled to hide. None of these "obstacles" kept them from screen stardom.

Byron M. "Bitsy" Grant made himself a top tennis player though barely over five feet tall. Herve Villechaize is an out-and-out midget—and co-star of a top-rated television show. Deformed dwarf Alexander Pope became one of England's greatest poets and most-sought-after society wits. Napoleon, despite his five-foot-three height, dominated the history of his time and conquered Europe.

"Three Finger" Brown had his right hand mangled in a childhood accident, yet succeeded in becoming a major-league pitcher and a baseball Hall-of-Famer, with the third-lowest earned-run average in the history of the game. Tom Dempsey was born with only half a right foot and two partial fingers on his right hand, yet became a pro-football player for the Philadelphia Eagles and in 1970 set a world record by kicking a sixty-three-yard field goal. Wilma Rudolph couldn't walk at the age of seven; in 1960 she became a triple Olympic gold medalist in track and field.

Theodore Roosevelt was a sickly, asthmatic child. Sheer guts and determination made him a two-fisted Western rancher and outdoor sportsman, a war hero who commanded the famed Rough Riders, and the most vigorous President in U.S. history.

But you say you suffer from a *real* physical handicap, which has cut you off from the outside world of accomplishment and left you a hopeless cripple?

Maybe you haven't heard that Franklin Delano Roosevelt was a polio victim who conducted his four presidential campaigns and led this country through two of the twentieth century's greatest crises—from a wheelchair.

The artist Toulouse-Lautrec, who gained fame by

painting the hectic night life of Paris, could get around only on wheeled boards. Charles Proteus Steinmetz, one of the world's foremost electrical engineers, active in both teaching and industry, was a hunchback.

Russian-American flier Alexander De Seversky, despite the loss of a leg, flew more than fifty combat missions and shot down thirteen enemy planes in World War I, then went on to become a test pilot and leading aeronautical engineer.

Jay J. Armes had both hands amputated after a childhood accident with dynamite. Yet he became a millionaire private detective, famous for never leaving a case unsolved, in the course of which he survived thirteen attempts on his life, using weapons concealed in his prostheses.

Even more severely handicapped was Frederick A. Fay, who found himself a quadriplegic as a result of a high-school gym accident. Undaunted, he earned a PhD in educational psychology, became director of research at Tufts University's New England Medical Center, founded Opening Doors, a counseling service for the disabled, and over the years has made himself not only an inspiring example but a leading spokesman for all handicapped people.

The loss of an eye might seem tragically incapacitating to some, but not to British Admiral Horatio Nelson, who saw the enemy fleet well enough to blow it away at Trafalgar, nor to Guglielmo Marconi, when he invented radio, nor to famed movie director John Ford and suave matinee idol Rex Harrison, nor to Israel's dashing, eye-patched war hero, statesman, and archeologist, Moshe Dayan, and certainly not to lovely, one-glass-eyed musical-comedy star Sandy Duncan, who recently scored a sensational Broadway hit in the title role in *Peter Pan*. Eric Hosking became a world-famed photographer of wild birds despite being similarly sight-handicapped.

The loss of one eye, of course, pales into insignificance

compared to the crushing misfortune of total blindness. Normally sighted folk cannot comprehend the impact of such a blow, which condemns the victim to a lifetime in the dark, unable to see the beauties of nature or the faces of his loved ones and fellow man, let alone the tools of whatever profession he may have hoped to pursue.

Yet the list of victims who have succeeded despite this massive handicap is fantastic. It includes blind computer expert James. R. Slagle, who became chief of the Hueristic Lab in the Division of Computer Research and Technology at the National Institutes of Health, and head of the Hueristics Group at the Lawrence Radiation Lab in California; Dr. David Hartman, who in 1976 became the first blind person ever to graduate from a U.S. medical school; blind musicians Ray Charles, Stevie Wonder, and Jose Feliciano; India-born journalist Ved Mehta and Argentina's Nobel-prize winning writer, Jorge Luis Borges.

Ludwig van Beethoven, often regarded as the greatest composer of all time, lost his hearing yet went on to write some of his greatest symphonies although stone deaf. Helen Keller overcame both blindness and deafness to gain world fame as a writer and lecturer. John Milton lost his sight but achieved towering greatness as a poet; his sonnet "On His Blindness" is considered one of the masterpieces of English literature.

You lack proper education and training, you say? That didn't stop Louie "Satchmo" Armstrong. P. T. Barnum never got past grade school yet became the world's greatest and richest showman. Leon Uris—whose parents were Russian-Jewish immigrants—flunked English three times and quit high school to join the Marines, then went on to become a best-selling author. His novel *Battle Cry,* by the way, was rejected twelve times before he found a publisher; eventually it became a motion picture.

Another high-school dropout was George Gershwin,

whom many consider America's greatest modern composer. Thomas Edison never even finished grade school—which didn't stop him from inventing the electric light, the phonograph, motion pictures, and a long enough list of other scientific firsts to rank him as one of the greatest inventors of all time.

One of America's top mail-order copywriters, Joe Sugarman of JS&A in Chicago, failed English in college and is now one of the highest-paid copywriters in the country.

Attorney Clarence Darrow, who won some of the most famous cases in American legal history, never attended law school.

Steven Spielberg's high-school grades were so poor that he couldn't get himself admitted to any major film school. Instead he bluffed his way onto movie-studio lots and learned his craft the hard way. His *Close Encounters of the Third Kind* is one of the top-grossing films of all time.

Wernher von Braun was a mathematical dunce in school before becoming Germany's top wartime rocket designer; later he helped launch America's space program. Albert Einstein's parents at first thought him retarded. At nine he spoke haltingly and answered questions only after long hesitation. On his first attempt to get admitted to Zurich's Polytechnic Institute, he flunked the entrance exams—then went on to formulate the theory of relativity, which revolutionized modern physics. Today he ranks with Newton and Darwin as an epoch-making scientific genius.

But maybe you regard your chief problem as psychological. Buckminster Fuller, you may be interested to know, was once on the verge of suicide. He pulled himself together and invented the architecturally dazzling geodesic dome and became a famed mathematical philosopher.

Ellen Glasgow's two serious romances ended unhappily, her brother took his own life, and she, too, attempted suicide before becoming a successful novelist. *In This Our*

Life, for which she won the Pulitzer prize in 1942, was written despite two successive heart attacks.

Marty Mann was herself an alcoholic before founding and becoming executive director of the National Council on Alcoholism. Her tireless efforts helped to save thousands from the ravages of that dread disease.

Author Somerset Maugham has told how, in his youth, he was so shy that when invited to a dinner party or other gathering he would sometimes walk the streets for an hour, trying to get up nerve enough to make an appearance. He became not only one of England's greatest modern novelists but also one of its most urbane and sought-after social lions—this despite a lifelong stammer.

Another shy stammerer was an ancient Greek named Demosthenes. He used to practice declaiming with stones in his mouth—and became the greatest orator in classical history.

Actress Elizabeth Ashley gained swift success in the 1960s—*too* swift, some might say—with the result that she suffered a nervous breakdown and was forced to retire from the stage. Despite these emotional pressures, she made a resounding comeback in the 1970s in such roles as Maggie in Tennessee Williams' *Cat on a Hot Tin Roof* and has since established herself as one of the outstanding actresses of the American theater.

You think you came from the wrong side of the tracks? Former U.S. Senator Mike Mansfield dropped out of school before the eighth grade, hopped freight cars across the country, and spent a night in jail. He was working as a shoveler in the Montana copper mines when his future wife persuaded him to complete his high-school education by taking correspondence courses. He became one of the most respected and influential lawmakers on Capitol Hill and, after retiring from the Senate, was appointed U.S. ambassador to Japan.

Leroy Garrett, as a black man, had an even tougher road to climb, coming out of the Alabama cotton fields to become owner and manager of radio station WEUP in Huntsville. He opened the station in 1958 in a converted house trailer. By the time of his death, twenty-two years later, his broadcasting complex covered more than eleven acres and had served as a training ground for many other broadcasters who, like himself, belonged to minority groups.

Sophia Loren was born not only poor but illegitimate. She was so skinny as a child that her schoolmates called her "Toothpick"; she suffered from mites and lice, as well as from nightmarish fears of the dark, stemming from times spent huddled in a crowded railway tunnel used as a wartime bomb shelter. From such squalid beginnings in her hometown near Naples, she blossomed into one of the most glamorous movie stars of her time.

Jovial Freddie Laker, who outgeneraled the major transatlantic airlines with his own cost-cutting Skytrain concept, grew up in poverty in London. His father mistreated the boy and later deserted the family—none of which kept Freddie from achieving fame and fortune as an aviation businessman.

Andrew Carnegie started life as a bobbin boy in a cotton factory, the son of a dirt-poor handloom weaver. He became a multimillionaire steel tycoon, whose vast philanthropies are still visible in, for example, the form of public libraries all over this country.

Adam Gimbel began as an immigrant backwoods pack peddler. Samuel Lord started out as an orphan boy sweating his livelihood in an English iron foundry. Today, Gimbels and Lord & Taylor are two of the most famous and successful department-store chains in the United States.

Ann Miller, the toast of Broadway as the star of *Sugar Babies*, began her glittering career at the age of eleven, dancing for coins in a tacky nightclub. Ralph Ellison, raised by a widowed mother who supported them by working as a domestic, surmounted poverty and prejudice against blacks to become a successful author; his novel *Invisible Man* won the National Book Award in 1953. Charlie Chaplin came out of the London slums to win worldwide fame and fortune as a movie comedian.

"All well and good," you say, "but it's too late for me—I'm too old" or "already a failure."

No kidding? Did you know that Truman failed as a haberdasher—and went on to become a Senator and President of the United States? Did you know that Erskine Caldwell had a hundred stories and novellas rejected and was forced to eke out a living as a hardscrabble potato farmer before *Tobacco Road* made him rich and famous? Did you know that Walt Disney's first production company went bankrupt? That business tycoon Cyrus Eaton lost $100 million in the Wall Street Crash and had to borrow money to start all over again? That R. H. Macy failed in six retailing tries before he opened the world-famous department store that brings you those charming Thanksgiving Day parades on television every year?

As for "too old," there are Colonel Sanders, who became a successful fast-food purveyor in his sixties; German chancellor Konrad Adenauer, who became leader of his country at the age of sixty-nine, during its most difficult postwar period; George Burns, who launched himself on an Oscar-winning movie career at the age of eighty; Grandma Moses, who became a famous painter in her eighties; Alberta Hunter, who scored a stunningly successful comeback as a blues singer at the age of eighty-two. At that same age, incidentally, after a life that would have exhausted most men years earlier, Winston Churchill began to write his best-selling *History of the English-Speaking Peoples.* At eighty-five Coco Chanel was still head of her Paris fashion house. At eighty-nine Harriet S. Adams is still turning out the *Nancy Drew* mysteries that have won her generations of fans. At ninety-one Adolf Zukor was chairman of Paramount Pictures—at the same age Eamon de Valera was serving as president of Ireland.

Marc Chagall at ninety-three is still painting. Composer Eubie Blake at ninety-eight is still playing to audiences regularly. Irving Berlin at ninety-two is still writing music. Composer Virgil Thomson is still working at eighty-four, as is Aaron Copland at eighty.

Artist Louise Nevelson is still very active at eighty. Eva Le Gallienne, eighty-one; Lillian Gish, eighty-three; Ruth Gordon, eighty-one; James Cagney, eighty-one; Helen Hayes, eighty; and Melvin Douglas, eighty, can still be seen on the stage, in movies, and on TV.

You can still hear Norman Vincent Peale preach at eighty-two. Lowell Thomas, who is eighty-eight, is still active. Albert Szent-Györgyi, who isolated vitamin C, at eighty-eight is still an active researcher.

If you think that your best work can come only when you are in your twenties and thirties, remember Johann von Goethe, who completed *Faust* between the ages of seventy-six and eighty-two; and Michelangelo, who created one of his most famous *Pietà*s at the age of seventy; and Douglas MacArthur, who was named commander of the UN forces in Korea at age seventy.

Frank Lloyd Wright created his legendary home in Arizona and the Price Tower in Oklahoma in his seventies and eighties, and Cecil B. De Mille made the movie *The Ten Commandments* at the age of seventy-five. Giuseppe Verdi began the opera *Falstaff* at age seventy-seven, and Golda Meir became Israel's prime minister at seventy. Laura I. Wilder, who didn't publish a book until age sixty-five, wrote many of her best children's stories after age seventy.

I could go on and on, of course, but is it really necessary?

Now, what were those dreadful obstacles and handicaps that have been holding you back from success all these years?

Welcome to the World of Lucky People.

4

All Luck Starts with an Idea

*I*deas have built empires and caused thrones to totter.

King George III lost his priceless American colonies because in the late 1700s the *idea* began to get around among the American colonists that taxation without representation is tyranny.

Not long afterward, King Louis XVI and his queen, Marie Antoinette, lost their thrones and their heads because the common people of France began to turn on to the *idea* of liberty, equality, fraternity.

Martin Luther King, Jr., led a modern crusade that helped to achieve full civil rights for black people because he and they took seriously the *idea* expressed in the U.S. Constitution that all men are created equal.

Tyrants and dictators have always tended to fear and mistrust intellectuals of all kinds for precisely that reason—because *ideas* can inspire people to take action and bring about revolutionary change. ("He thinks too much: such men are dangerous," as Shakespeare put it in his play *Julius Caesar*.)

The tightest censorship in the world today is maintained by the Kremlin bosses of the Soviet Union because they understand all too well the explosive power of *ideas.*

Ideas are equally important to your own success in life because, as the title of this chapter states, all luck starts with an idea.

You may respond impatiently, "Okay, but what do you mean by 'an idea'? That's too vague. *What* idea?"

Good question—especially since there's more than one kind of idea that may play an important role in your personal success story.

Let me cite an example.

A quarter of a century ago, a seven-year-old boy was at home when an important-looking stranger carrying a black bag called at his house. Someone in the household was ill. The stranger looked in briefly on the sick person and uttered a few words of advice to the boy's mother.

She listened attentively—obviously much impressed—then took out her purse and gave him ten dollars.

The visit had lasted only a few minutes. And for this his mother had paid the man ten dollars—not to mention her having treated him with such great respect.

After the stranger had gone, the boy asked her, "Who was that man?"

"That was the doctor, dear," she replied.

Whereupon the boy exclaimed, "When I grow up, *I'm* going to be a doctor."

And those were no idle words, believe me. From that day on, the whole course of his life was decided. His determination to become a doctor never wavered. Everything was subordinated to that one *fixed idea* or motivation.

He studied hard in high school, taking all the available science courses, had no trouble gaining admission to an academically top-ranked university, and went on to medical school. Today he's a doctor practicing in Columbus,

Ohio. Every time we go there, I josh him about his reasons for studying medicine—because that physician happens to be my thirty-two-year-old nephew.

The kind of fixed idea, or ambition, that propels us toward a goal can perhaps best be called a dream—in the sense that Martin Luther King, Jr., intended when he uttered that famous line at the Lincoln Memorial: "I have a dream. . . ."

Very often people say it's easy to get ahead if you have a famous or influential father. That may be true, but all my friends who had rich fathers and ready-made businesses were envious of me for having made it on my own. No matter how much they increased the size of their father's business, they always felt they could not have gotten their first break had they started from scratch without parental help.

I may or may not qualify as a famous or influential father, but my own two children are living examples of the fact that no outside help is needed if a person is truly determined to make his or her own luck.

Steve early on had the ambition to become a writer and journalist. When he got his master's degree from Medill, the school of journalism at Northwestern University, he might well have come to me for an inside break, since I knew many publishers and editors. Instead he followed up a bulletin-board notice that said:

WANTED

Graduate willing to work for slave wages.

He called for an interview, got the job—which was with a top magazine in Chicago—and in two years rose from office hack to a by-lined position as the magazine's articles editor. Luck? No—he worked many a night till midnight to meet deadlines and get his job done.

Louise graduated from Vassar with a BA in the humanities—and no working skills. A round of employment agencies quickly showed her the bleak outlook for inexperienced office help. What to do? Try to cash in on her father's contacts and influence to land some secure, undemanding job?

That wasn't Louise's way. She was determined to create her own breaks. She saw an ad for a paralegal with a law firm at a salary of $125 a week. At the time this was a brand-new occupation with duties that consisted of organizing cases, digesting briefs, and doing the general backup work that was once performed by law clerks before inflation made them too expensive to hire for this work.

The pay was minimal—but Louise saw the opening as a challenge and an opportunity. She answered the ad, landed the job (with a prestigious old law firm), and later moved on to a more dynamic, faster-growing firm that specialized in a wide range of corporate law, becoming that firm's first paralegal. Today, nine years later, she heads the largest paralegal staff in the country, with administrative responsibility for over 125 people. Luck? No—she worked her tail off often through the night and often seven days a week.

I remember reading somewhere how Zane Grey, an Ohio-born dentist practicing in New York, who had never been west of the Mississippi, was obsessed by the dream of becoming a novelist—perhaps because he loved to imagine himself as a cowboy having exciting adventures. His first efforts were rejected by publisher after publisher, until the wife of one happened to read a manuscript by Grey and urged her husband to publish it.

Never was wifely advice more wisely heeded. Grey became America's most famous and best-loved author of Western adventure yarns, including such unforgettable epics as *Riders of the Purple Sage, The Lone Star Ranger, The Wan-*

derer of the Wasteland, and others, many of which have been turned into equally successful motion pictures.

Most hotel bars and pubs look alike, but hotelkeeper Malcolm Green in North London came up with a new idea that would bring in more customers than his competitors had. He put up a sign that said that his pub would permit no smoking, no jukeboxes, and no one-armed bandits. He realized that ecology-minded customers would like to drink in peace and nonpollution, and soon his pub was thriving. Was Green lucky to make his bar successful? No. He did something—not an invention—not a new drink—but an awareness that there is a new crowd, aborning—a drinking, nonsmoking crowd, whose numbers are growing.

You, too, need this kind of *idea* or *dream* to fire your imagination and goad you onward to success. That's why in a previous chapter I urged you to decide exactly what you want out of life—whether it's to become a qualified commercial pilot, captaining your own jetliner; a ballet star; a hit with the opposite sex; a wealthy inventor, or something much more down to earth but just as satisfying, such as the proprietor of your own small business or a housewife fattening the family budget with extra income earned through successful spare-time activities.

Having your sights fixed on that definite goal is an all-important first step toward success.

The next step, of course, is figuring out how to achieve that goal. And this is where an entirely different kind of idea comes in—or, rather, becomes absolutely essential.

Do you ever read the funny papers? If so, in some comic strip or other, you must surely have seen a character with an electric light bulb flashing on in a thought cloud over his head.

That bulb lighting up, of course, indicates that the character has just had a great idea about how to accomplish something.

And that's the kind of idea *you* need at this point.

Again, let me give you some examples.

Let's say you're a poor kid in New York. You'd love to go to summer camp in the Catskills. But it costs two hundred dollars—which is two hundred bucks more than your parents can afford. True, the guy who runs the camp will let some of the older kids come free as waiters. But he picks those lucky dogs only from among the kids who have gone in previous summers for the regular fee.

What to do? ... That was once *my* problem because I was that kid.

Well, I brooded over the situation for several days, wishing like crazy that I could come up with some solution so that I, too, could enjoy the fun of summer camp and get my fair share of all that fresh air and green woods and sparkling blue lake water to splash around in.

Then I had an idea.

I proposed to the camp owner that he let the waiters come at half price, which they could earn back out of their tips. The notion had never even occurred to him. Sounded terrific—but would it work? Would parents actually pay a hundred dollars for their kids to be camp waiters?

I proved they would—by going out and rounding up fifteen of my friends and acquaintances who were eager to go to camp on those terms. In exchange, I got to go as a waiter myself—free—even though I'd never gone before as a paying camper.

Thus, my *idea* earned the camp owner fifteen hundred dollars that he never expected—and won *me* a summer vacation in the mountains, far from the steaming concrete jungle.

This was the first time I came up with an idea of the kind I call "common sense," and it made money for someone else. Of course I also benefited from the idea—and that's the whole point. It was a case of *making my own luck.*

I believe that everyone has this innate ability but doesn't always know how to use it.

All that's required is thinking, How can this situation be of value to me in getting what I want? This is not the same as using people. This is being alert, attentive, and aware of opportunities. Such opportunities exist all the time—everywhere. My life story is an illustration of this fact.

At the time I got out of college the Great Depression was still dragging on, and World War II was already looming on the horizon. I noticed a sign posted telling of a job available at the state office building. The salary was only forty dollars a month, but to me, in those days, that sounded like a fortune, so I applied. You can imagine my delight when I was hired.

The job consisted of managing a small credit union for state employees. The credit union, in effect, operated like a small bank. Our clientele ranged from clerks to commissioners. I made a point of getting to know everyone on a friendly basis. One day I read in the newspaper that factories in New York State were having trouble in filling job openings, and therefore in meeting their production quotas, because of the war.

Frieda S. Miller, who was then commissioner of labor, was one of our depositors. Next time she came in, I mentioned the article I'd read. She replied that it was a very complex problem. Labor unions wouldn't send members of racial minorities to apply for jobs on the grounds that they were always rejected. Factory owners, in turn, pleaded as their excuse that none ever applied, so how could they hire any?

A council was to be formed, and I suggested that, instead of merely appointing a representative of industry and a representative of labor, she appoint the president of a company who was known *not* to hire blacks and to appoint the head of the union that had the contract with this company. Sitting them both down at a table, we would be able to prevent management from saying we won't hire blacks because the union won't send them, and to prevent the union from saying we won't send blacks because management won't hire them.

She recognized the suggestion as a good one, and one that would put them on the spot and serve as a lesson for others. As a result I was asked to become director of research for the council.

And the good luck I'd made for myself didn't stop there. In the course of serving on the council, I eventually met many prominent business and labor leaders who were later instrumental in advancing my career. Moreover, the council itself had some important spin-off dividends. Through this agency I helped bring about the passage of the first antidiscrimination law in the United States. I was also able to promote the passage of a bill that established at Cornell University the first school of labor and industrial relations.

This in turn led to my participation in another university-based project—which in time involved me in various fund-raising activities and eventually propelled me into the field of public relations.

All this because of one simple, commonsense *idea* that none of the experts in the field had thought of. Study the problem and use your common sense to solve it simply.

Now let me give you an altogether different sort of example, involving both love and career.

From time to time, you may have read or heard about how some young man has advertised his love for his girlfriend in a spectacular way designed not only to catch her eye but to capture her heart. It's the type of story that seems to crop up periodically, like the latest report of somebody trying to immortalize himself in the Guinness Book of Records by attempting to break the domino-toppling or roller-coaster–endurance record.

I happen to know personally about one of those spectacular romantic advertisers via a mutual acquaintance.

The young man in this particular case—I'll call him Bert—was head over heels in love with a beautiful girl named Sandra. He wanted to marry her, but she was undecided—for several reasons, including the fact that a more prosperous rival was also on the verge of proposing to her, whereas poor Bert was about to be laid off from his present job in the advertising department of a clothing chain and so far had been unsuccessful in landing a hoped-for job with a certain ad agency.

What did he do? Maybe you've guessed it. He rented billboard space at a spot that Sandra passed on her way to work every morning. In huge, Day-Glo lettering he spelled out his proposal:

> DEAREST SANDRA:
> I LOVE YOU TO DISTRACTION!
> WILL YOU MARRY ME?
> YOURS FOREVER,
> XXXXX BERT

His billboard love letter got front-page coverage in the local newspaper (and not by chance, incidentally, but because Bert made a point of tipping off a news photographer). In addition to this local publicity, the story was also picked up by the wire services.

How could Sandra turn a cold shoulder to such a spectacular and passionate plea—especially with the whole city awaiting her answer to Bert's proposal? His rival was upstaged. Not only that, but the advertising agency to which Bert had applied for a position as copywriter could hardly help but be impressed by the sales and publicity flair of this particular job applicant.

Bert got a yes from his lady love and an invitation from the ad agency to start work the next Monday morning. It would be cynical, I suppose, to suggest that his billboard ploy was just as carefully calculated to land him that job as it was to win Sandra's heart, but the fact is it did just that.

One more example: A friend of mine, Mrs. Sylvia Stoner, who lives in Manhattan, got a phone call in the spring of 1980 from a cousin living in Dubuque. The two had been extremely close during girlhood and college, but in recent years had rarely seen each other.

"When are you coming to see us?" Sylvia asked.

"Oh, we'd love to," came the reply. "As a matter of fact, Hank's got next week off and we actually did consider flying to New York. But have you any idea what rooms are gong for now? The cheapest we could locate costs sixty dollars a night. I'm afraid that's more than we can afford, added to the cost of the plane tickets."

Sylvia herself would have been only too glad to have them stay with her, but she and her husband and their two teenage sons occupied a two-bedroom apartment, with hardly a square foot of extra space.

The conversation was almost over when an idea suddenly occurred to her. "Wait before you make up your mind definitely not to come, Betty," she exclaimed. "I may be able to find you a room in one of my friends' homes a lot cheaper than sixty dollars a night. Let me call you back after I check."

It took Sylvia only three calls to find a friend who had a pleasant house in Brooklyn, just across the East River, and who was delighted at a chance to earn twenty dollars a night by renting out an unused bedroom. What was more, both the bedding and the room itself were spotlessly clean and free of insect life, unlike all too many hotel rooms now being offered to the public in the Big Apple.

Needless to say, both Betty and her husband were also delighted at the chance to visit and spend a week in New York City so cheaply and conveniently.

That incident stuck firmly in Sylvia Stoner's mind. The more she thought about it, the more obvious it seemed.

An electric light bulb flashed on in her mind.

There must be a good many people, businessmen and others, who would love to come to New York if they could do so assured in advance of finding a reasonable, comfortable room. In fact Sylvia's own husband, who was in the garment business, knew of a good many such cases—out-of-town buyers who were sometimes forced to cancel visits to fashion shows just because of the difficulty of finding a suitable hotel room.

Just for the heck of it, Sylvia decided to test her idea. She made a list of all the people she knew in New York who *might* be willing to rent out rooms in their own homes, either regularly or occasionally, provided they could be assured of the trustworthiness of their guests.

To Sylvia's amazement, she scored on almost 80 percent of her tries.

At that moment she realized she had the nucleus of a successful business. Through her husband and other contacts, including various travel agencies and business firms, she began offering to find rooms for travelers at lower-than-commercial hotel rates, in Manhattan and the other boroughs of New York City. Orders came pouring in.

Within months Sylvia did, indeed, have a going business. By the time of the Democratic Convention in New York in August, she was able to provide rooms for more than a hundred delegates and, needless to add, at a fair but pleasant profit for herself.

* * *

Let's stop for a moment and think about those four examples I've given you so far—namely, my own experiences relative to summer camp and with the industry-labor advisory council, Bert's billboard marriage proposal, and Sylvia Stoner's room-hunting enterprise.

Each one involved an *idea*—an electric light bulb flashing on in someone's head. And, as you may have noticed, each one also involved finding the answer to a problem.

The *idea* provided the *answer.*

Those are the kinds of ideas I want *you* to start working on when I say that *all luck starts with an idea.*

Don't tell me you're no good at thinking up ideas. It's not all that hard. In fact it's downright easy!

No doubt you've heard that old jingle "Find a pin and pick it up; all the day you'll have good luck." Well, potentially profitable or luck-making ideas are lying all around you, like pins on the floor, just *waiting* to be picked up. All you have to do is open your eyes and *see* them.

But we'll go into all that in the next chapter. For the moment I want you to realize two things: (1) what I told you in the title of this chapter—namely, all luck *does* start with an idea, and (2) the kind of idea I'm talking about is a *problem-solving idea.*

Now let's take a closer look at our four examples.

In the first one, my problem was that I wanted to go to summer camp but my parents couldn't afford it. I solved the problem by offering the camp owner a money-making idea, in exchange for which he let me come free as a camper waiter.

In the second example, the New York State commissioner of labor was faced with a problem that not only affected many individuals but also was slowing down the state's war effort. I helped her by coming up with the *idea* of forming an advisory council of labor and industry. In return, she appointed me to a position on the council and thereby opened up an avenue of recognition that advanced my future career in important ways.

In the third example, Bert was faced with both a love problem and a job problem. He licked both with the single *idea* of a billboard marriage proposal. This solved his first problem by dramatically demonstrating to his sweetheart the magnitude and intensity of his love for her; she was so thrilled that she agreed to marry him. It solved his other problem as well by demonstrating just as dramatically to his hoped-for future employer that he had advertising talent and pizzazz of a kind that could help to earn them new business, and they gave him the job he was after.

In the fourth example, my friend Mrs. Sylvia Stoner— a typical, average housewife—solved a friend's problem by finding her and her husband a room in a private home. Sylvia, let me hasten to point out, was not at first pursuing any selfish purpose, aside from the prospective pleasure of seeing her old friend again. Yet deep down, like many other housewives, she had sometimes cherished daydreamy thoughts of an independent career—or at least of earning extra household money through some sort of spare-time activity. She didn't even realize at first that she had accidentally stumbled on an *idea* for accomplishing just that. But when she did, she seized her opportunity with both hands and proceeded to make the most of it.

Now, notice two things. None of these ideas involved anything more than simple common sense. None of them required any special genius or know-how. Given a little time and reflection, *you* could have come up with them just as easily as the next person. True, Bert's idea was a bit out of the ordinary, but what it took more than genius was sheer nerve or brass—the willingness to step out of the crowd and brazenly call attention to yourself.

Second, they all involved giving something to or doing

something for somebody else. And in each case this resulted in a *benefit to the giver.*

I showed the camp owner how to make more money.
The result was a summer at camp, free, for myself.

I showed the commissioner of labor how to cope with
an urgent industrial problem. The result was an upward
boost to my own career.

Bert gave his girlfriend dramatic assurance of his deep
love, and his prospective employer dramatic assurance that
he would be an asset to their business. The result was that
he won both a wife and the hoped-for job.

Sylvia did her friend a favor, and by doing so created
a profitable spare-time business for herself.

This, too, is an important ingredient of the kinds of
ideas you need to make your own luck. By doing something for others, you accomplish something for yourself. By
fulfilling the needs or wants of others, you thereby fulfill
your own needs or wants.

You might almost call this an application of the Gold-
en Rule.

To sum up, to make your own luck or success, you
must start with an *idea.*

Let's say you want to make more money, start your
own business, make yourself loved by others, or, win a job
promotion. In short, you *want* something from somebody—
your boss, the public, your wife, or your acquaintances.

Your problem is *how to get* that something.

Your idea should provide a solution to the problem—
by doing something for or giving something to that other
person or persons from whom you want something in return.

In the next chapter I'll show you where to look for and
find those all-important ideas.

5

Where to Look for Ideas

Probably everyone has read stories about people stumbling on treasure in their own backyards. Just recently there was a newspaper report of an English farmer plowing up a little golden figure in his oat field. It turned out to be a pre-Roman relic over two thousand years old, which museum experts pronounced priceless.

And did you know that one of the biggest diamonds ever found in South Africa was accidentally kicked up out of the dirt by a little boy romping with his friends?

I personally know of a woman who, with her sister, was going over a pile of odds and ends that had once belonged to their father. Some of it had been cleaned out of his desk at the time of his death, years before, then shoved aside and forgotten. Among the rest of the "junk" they discovered a box crammed full of ten- and twenty-dollar gold pieces.

All sorts of valuable art objects, stamps, books, manuscripts, and the like have been found in much the same way—because someone took the trouble to *notice* and examine things that everyone else had overlooked.

In your local library you're almost certain to find one or more volumes telling you how to mine your own attic for valuable antiques.

Would you call a person lucky who discovers hidden treasure right in his own home?

Well, listen closely because I have an important secret to impart: This can happen to you.

But, let me hasten to add, only if you're smart enough to *notice* what may be lying right under your nose or staring you right in the face.

For example, where are you sitting right now as you read this book.

In the living room? . . . Okay, what do you see as you look around? Your TV set, perhaps. Does that suggest anything?

Let me tell you about a guy named Danny Browne who was sitting in his living room one evening, watching his TV set. The picture quality wasn't too good, which was depressing because Danny was in no position just then to shell out a wad of cash for repairs—maybe even including an expensive new picture tube. The set was too old to sink that much money into, anyhow.

Actually, Danny had been hankering for a long time to invest in a new twenty-three-inch color model. But where could he lay hands on that kind of bread without digging into savings? To make things even more frustrating, the Super Bowl was coming up next week—and Danny was a rabid football fan.

No doubt it was that latter fact that eventually gave him his big idea. If he couldn't afford to buy a new color set, maybe he could rent one. But when he checked out the situation by looking in the Yellow Pages and making inquiries, he learned there was no television rental service in his neighborhood.

That's when an electric light bulb flashed on in Danny's head. If there was no local TV rental service, he mused, why not start one?

Danny Browne did, and today he's running a successful TV-rental business—with three stores. I know all this because not long ago I rented a set from Danny and happened to ask how he got started.

Glance once again, if you will, at that question I asked a few paragraphs back: Where are you sitting right now as you read this book?

Maybe you're not sitting in the living room, as Danny was. Maybe you're comfortably settled out in the backyard in a lawn chair. Okay, look around—and keep your eyes wide open.

How's the grass coming up? Not too well? Well, sure—maybe the soil's too poor and rocky. Of course if you had a roto-tiller and could really turn up the soil, then add the right kind of nutrients and seed, that would be a different story. Then you could develop a really lush green carpet of lawn. The only catch is, all that would take time and effort, more than you're prepared to expend at this moment.

On the other hand, as you look around, maybe your neighbors could use the same kind of lawn treatment. And if you rented a roto-tiller for your own yard, maybe you could do theirs, too, while you're at it—all for a nice fat fee, of course.

That's the kind of thinking that led to Lawn King and similiar franchise businesses. It's also the kind of thinking that led a high-school kid named Joey Magruder to start his own successful lawn-care service last year.

It was still early spring when that electric light bulb flashed on in Joey's head. He was about to graduate from high school, and he knew it would be no snap to find a job. Instead of waiting till mid-June, Joey got moving in April.

First he canvassed the neighborhood for blocks around, noting the addresses of all the houses with lawns that needed intensive improvement. Then he tramped around after school and on weekends, ringing doorbells and asking householders if they'd like their lawns reseeded and fertilized.

By dint of pounding shoe leather and refusing to be discouraged by turn-downs, he lined up enough customers to justify renting the necessary equipment. And by purchasing the seed and fertilizer in quantity, he was able to talk the local hardware-store proprietor into granting him a bargain rate. What's more, he didn't stop there. He made sure each job was done to the customer's satisfaction—and he'd also stop by later to see if the seed was sprouting, at which time he'd ask if the customer would like to hire him for weekly lawn cutting and periodic refertilizing.

More than half his customers did rehire him, and today, more than a year later, Joey is no longer worried about finding a job. He's built up his own thriving little lawn-care business, which he varies seasonally by leaf raking in autumn and snow shoveling and driveway plowing in winter—and all the while he's putting himself through a local community college with his own earnings.

How can you stop a kid like that?

But let's move on to the bedroom. . . .

One day Ruth Grosstetter finished her housewifely chores for the afternoon, soaked in the tub for a while, and then settled down patiently to give herself a manicure and a pedicure before going to pick up her husband at the station when he returned from work.

Ruth was artistic enough (if that's the word) to enjoy painting her nails. All the same, it did take a certain amount of tedious effort and concentration, not to mention occasional contortion when she pretzeled herself into position to do her toenails. And she found herself thinking how nice it would be if she could just relax *and let someone else* do it all for her

At that moment an electric light bulb flashed on in Ruth's head.

Now, the Grosstetters are solid citizens, but not quite solid enough for Ruth to afford the services of a professional manicurist, let alone one who'd make house calls. And neither are most of their neighbors. But suppose one of the women on her block was willing to drop around and do her friends' nails on call for, say, a modest five dollars.

Ruth herself would certainly have been willing to pay for such a convenient service, and she was reasonably certain most of the other women would, too. So why not offer to do it herself, as a way of picking up some extra household money? No reason to feel embarrassed or self-conscious about it, either; more than half the local housewives were already working at part-time jobs to augment their husbands' paychecks.

Ruth's spare-time business became an overnight success. Not only did her customers enjoy a feeling of pampered luxury at being manicured in the comfort of their own homes, they also enjoyed the opportunity to have a long, satisfying woman-to-woman chat with a friend and neighbor. Before long, she branched out into washing and setting hair and giving home permanents. Today Ruth is able to add fifty to eighty dollars a week to the Grosstetters' household budget—all because she had a bright idea one afternoon while sitting in her bedroom doing her nails.

Equally important, of course, is that she *acted on her idea.*

Why have I gone through this room-to-room tour-of-the-house routine? Certainly not because your home is the only place to look for ideas. Far from it. That brilliant electric light bulb can flash on in your head anytime, anyplace—provided you keep your eyes and ears and mind wide open for valuable impressions and insights.

The main reason for the room-to-room bit was to cite examples of how to use specific real-life objects and activities—like your television set or your lawn or doing your nails—as thought starters and luck makers.

There was once a famous pulp-magazine writer named Arthur J. Burks, whose boast was that he could take any object and make a story out of it. An interviewer (for *Reader's Digest*, as I recall) once tested him by pointing to a doorknob. Burks went into a trance and soon came up with the plot for a detective story featuring a cache of stolen diamonds that were hidden in the hollow interior of a doorknob. The interviewer tiptoed away as the slow *tap-tap* of Burks's typewriter increased to a noisy, high-speed clatter.

You can use the same gimmick when you prospect for luck-making ideas. If you simply sit down and let your mind wander, you're apt to find yourself woolgathering and daydreaming and eventually doze off. But by focusing your thoughts on specific *things* or *activities*, you'll generally find you can churn out more and better ideas faster.

On the other hand, don't let me leave you with the mistaken impression that ideas will come only when you're actively looking for them. No, indeed. Some of your best and most profitable notions may strike you at wholly unexpected moments once you acquire the habit of looking at the world through "lucky" lenses. When that happens, your mind automatically and subconsciously screens and scrutinizes everything that passes across its field of awareness for a possible luck-making angle or potential. Once you've gotten the knack, your mind will tend to retain the kinds of ideas you can turn to profitable use.

Or think of yourself as a 'Forty-niner panning for gold.

The things you see going on all around you are like the swirling sands of the riverbed. You shake 'em up and wash away the worthless lightweight grains, and the glitter you see shining up at you from the bottom of the pan will be the heavier particles of gold—the profitable ideas that can help to *make you lucky.*

For example, one Saturday morning last spring, a young woman friend of ours and her husband drove to a nearby town where a flea market is held every weekend. They had never gone to a flea market before, and to Nora it was an eye-opening experience.

She found herself particularly noticing a girl who looked no older than twenty or twenty-one, and who was offering for sale an assortment of sweaters and T-shirts and Indian cotton blouses. The girl seemed utterly relaxed and was idly plucking a mandolin as the human tide of gawkers and shoppers ebbed and flowed around the flea market. Yet every time Nora happened to look at her, she seemed to be chatting up another customer or closing a sale. And a similar rate of business was going on at most of the other stalls in the market.

Nora finally went up and asked the girl how she had gone about staking out stall space. "No problem—I rented it from the manager," was the reply. And where had she gotten her stock? "From a wholesaler, naturally."

Nora was more fascinated than ever. Good heavens, she thought, was going into business for yourself all that easy?

Before leaving, she searched out the owner-manager of the market lot. "How much to rent a stall?" she asked. "Fifty bucks for the weekend," said the manager. "But all that gets you is space. You have to set up your own stand or back a van into position and use the tailgate to display your goods."

Nora promptly wrote him a check for fifty dollars.

As she drove off with her husband her mind was already busy making plans. The following Friday, she visited three wholesalers and put together an attractive assortment of aprons and housedresses and gaily patterned napkins and tablecloths. At nine o'clock the next morning she was in business.

By the end of the weekend Nora had taken in over four hundred dollars, against an expense of less than two hundred and fifty dollars. Within a month or so she had expanded to three stalls, displaying inexpensive children's wear in one and hand-crafted costume jewelry in another, and had hired two high-school girls to help her.

Thanks to her keen eye for merchandise and her instinct for what will please the public taste, Nora is now operating a thriving business—and she's never had so much fun before. Her life has taken on a whole new dimension—all because she kept her eyes and her mind open, and was quick to react to a stimulating new experience.

As I've said before, and will say again and again in the course of this book, ideas are all around you. All you need to do is be alert and receptive. And once you've latched onto an idea, do something about it.

Everyone since the beginning of the human race has seen rocks lying on the ground. But one man saw those plain little old hunks of stone—and got the idea for Pet Rocks. And then he proceeded to make a fortune out of his inspiration.

When Mount Saint Helens exploded in the state of Washington, sending thousands of tons of volcanic ash flying through the air, a young man in New Jersey got an idea. This was a memorable historic event. Maybe, he thought, people would *pay* for souvenirs of that event—in other words, for samples of that ash.

Sound crazy? We should all be that crazy. He got relatives to collect the stuff, then advertised it—and orders came pouring in.

Incidentally—just to get rid of another possible misapprehension—don't get the idea that you must always rely on your own private observations and experiences as a source of ideas. *Take an interest in people.* Don't just shake hands limply and mutter a perfunctory how-do-you-do. Talk to them, prod them for information about themselves and their work—and above all *listen* to what they have to say.

Some time back, in the course of talking to various newspaper editors, I asked them what was the most popular feature in their papers. To a man, they all said, "The astrology column." Yet none of those columns offered anything beyond the vaguest, broadest generalities—the sort of platitudinous advice that could apply to almost anyone who happened to pick up the newspaper that day.

Why? Because in all the thousands of years that people have been practicing astrology, no one had ever found a way to compute individual horoscopes on a mass-production basis. Yet why shouldn't that be possible in this modern era of high-speed computers, capable of performing a mind-boggling array of complicated mathematical operations in a second?

Everyone to whom I put this suggestion assured me it could not be done. Nevertheless, the possibility continued to intrigue me, and I consulted leading astrologers all over the world, as well as various computer-programming experts. Eventually I was able to develop a system of computerized astrology.

The point I wish to make here is that in time I built that computerized system into a million-dollar-a-year business—even though I knew nothing about astrology or computers—all because I kept my ears open when talking to newspaper editors and found out what their readers went for most avidly.

Even though you may not be able to glean a specific luck-making idea from a given person, it may still be worth your while to listen to what he has to say. In nearly every success story there is at least the germ of an idea or principle that can be applied usefully to your own case.

Recently I checked into a Manhattan hospital for a physical examination. My roommate was a young, smart, energetic Puerto Rican New Yorker. He turned out to be a building contractor—a most unusual profession for a young man fresh out of the *barrio* with no more than a high-school education.

I asked him how he happened to get into that line of work. He told me there were gutted, vandalized, abandoned tenement buildings all over his neighborhood in Brooklyn. With living space at a premium, and whole families crowded into tiny, squalid apartments, it seemed criminal to let such buildings stand vacant and go to rack and ruin.

With admirable gumption and energy, Juan got permission from the city authorities to restore the gutted structures and let them out to deserving families who would undertake to maintain them and pay for the necessary utilities. Then he hustled around to suppliers and talked them into letting him have the building materials he needed on credit, to be paid for once the buildings started generating rent.

Even at this point his efforts were derided as hopeless and ridiculous. There was no possible way to guard the building materials once they were delivered to the tenement sites. The street gangs, he was told, would steal him blind and vandalize the buildings all over again as soon as they were repaired.

But Juan refused to be discouraged. Instead of waiting for trouble to happen, he went straight to the gang leaders and sought their help. The buildings, he pointed out, were being repaired for the sake of their own families—for their own people. They themselves had a personal stake in the upgrading of their own neighborhood. Would they and their fellow gang members volunteer to help guard the building materials until they could be put to use?

The street gangs did much more than merely serve as guards. For once someone was talking sense to them, man to man—talking their own language and in terms of their own self-interest. As a result the gang members not only guarded the building materials—they even pitched in on the repair work. And as they learned the skills and crafts of the building trades on the job, by actual do-it-yourself experience, Juan was also learning the skills and know-how of the building contractor.

Within three years he was no longer just a public-spirited unemployed block leader. He had developed into a financially successful contractor; and with his example and inspiration, ghetto youngsters with no future had trained themselves as skilled, employable craftsmen.

It's true that I derived no specific ideas from my conversations with Juan that I could apply to my own business. But quite aside from the inspirational value of his story, let me give you two important tips that are illustrated by his example.

First, at the very outset, Juan's project was threatened by a serious *obstacle*—namely, the likelihood that lawless street gangs would steal his building supplies and wreck his work as fast as it was completed.

Instead of letting himself be stopped or thwarted or intimidated by this obstacle, he tackled it squarely and turned it into a positive advantage. As a result the menacing street gangs helped to safeguard and carry through a project they might otherwise have destroyed.

This is a principle (and a tip) I can't emphasize too strongly: *When boldly faced, obstacles can be turned into advantages.*

Examples of this abound in almost every success story you read. It almost seems to be a principle of nature, just as broken bones, when they heal, tend to be thicker at the fracture point—as if nature were trying to make the bone stronger so as to resist similar breaks in the future, the same way welders "beef up" a broken structural member with extra metal when they weld two broken parts together.

A young friend of mine, who works in a local clothing store, was assigned the responsibility for inventory control. Almost at once he found the job too big and sprawling to handle. The main reason was that there was simply no way to assert control as soon as the garments arrived at the store. Vans and drivers, he found out, are too expensive to sit around idly waiting on store procedures. Because of this, instead of the garments being checked over and tagged on the spot, they had to be unloaded fast and carted off to the proper department—suits, sport coats, slacks, outerwear, shirts. And, of course, before he could get around to each department to process the individual items, they would get mixed in with the rest of the stock, and some would quickly be sold or, worse yet, ripped off in ways that could seldom be traced.

Instead of letting the problem floor him, my friend talked the store manager into letting him use a small refuse and storage room for purposes of inventory control. He rolled up his sleeves, cleaned up the room, and personally installed pipe racks. Thereafter, when a truckload of garments arrived, they were first unloaded and hung at this reception point. Here he could check them against the manifest and tag each item properly, so that its subsequent disposal would automatically be recorded and later verified by regular computer procedures.

Thus, he not only overcame the obstacle that was facing him; he solved the store's inventory-control headache so swiftly and effectively that he earned the manager's enthusiastic appreciation and won himself a prompt promotion.

Still another example is the case history of Ruth Handler, the indomitable lady who co-founded the immensely successful Mattel toy company and created the fabulous Barbie doll. At the same time in her life that she found herself faced with stunning business reverses and ultimate corporate disaster, Mrs. Handler had to undergo a mastectomy.

The loss of a breast—which to most women would be like losing their femininity—might well have come as the final crushing blow, especially when she learned to her dismay that good breast prostheses simply didn't exist. But instead of going down for the count, Ruth Handler threw herself wholeheartedly into the job of developing a truly well-fitting artificial breast in a variety of sizes.

As a result—by turning an obstacle into an advantage—she has now formed a new corporation to produce and market the artificial breast, called Nearly Me, and thus at an age when most people are moving toward retirement, she has launched herself on a whole new career.

In short, the *idea* for her successful new business came automatically when she boldly tackled and overcame an apparently overwhelming obstacle.

Going back to the case of Juan, the Hispanic building contractor, let me draw your attention to a second important point. He didn't start the project of repairing those gutted buildings with the express intention and ambition of becoming a building contractor. What he was trying to do was improve his neighborhood and thus help other people of his own ethnic background.

In doing so, he also achieved a personal, successful career.

Thus, once again we see illustrated that prime luck-making principle (and my second tip): *By helping others, you will also help yourself to success.*

Or, to state the same principle in a slightly different fashion, to find your own luck-making ideas, look for ways to help others.

In the last chapter I described luck-making ideas as problem-solving ideas.

And, as we've just seen, luck-making ideas can also be characterized as ideas for helping others.

Now let's put it a third way: All of us have needs and desires. And, provided we have money or something equally valuable and negotiable, we are universally inclined to expend it on fulfilling those needs and desires.

So another way to prospect for luck-making or money-making ideas is to look for ways to satisfy people's needs and desires.

Again, Ruth Handler's case offers a perfect example. By researching the problem thoroughly, she learned that 80,000 mastectomies are performed annually in this country, and that there are probably two million women in the United States who have lost one or both breasts. She knew all too well how desperately those women yearn to restore their natural shape.

By developing a product that fulfills that yearning, Mrs. Handler has now zoomed aloft on a new and successful career.

Our friend Juan's fiancée, by the way, came to visit him at the hospital. She was a bright, attractive young woman who was employed as a paralegal assistant by a fast-rising team of young lawyers who specialized in representing illegal aliens facing trouble with the U.S. immigration authorities.

They had taken on their first such case, she told me, as a favor—only to find themselves swamped by dozens of similar individuals frantically in need of legal counsel. And suddenly they realized that here was a whole untapped area of law practice. Now, within the space of less than three years, those two young attorneys—neither of whom had graduated from a prestigious law school or started out with any great expectations of making much money—have their schedules crammed with clients, and are earning far more than a lot of top-ranking Harvard or Yale Law School graduates who are lucky enough to land jobs in the snootiest Park Avenue law firms.

All this because they undertook to serve someone's special needs—as a personal favor.

Juan himself, of course, is a Hispanic whose drive and energy have quickly launched him on the road to success. An even more dramatic example is Manuel Villafana of Arden Hills, Minnesota, who has already established two fantastically successful firms manufacturing electronic heart pacemakers.

It goes without saying that such pacemakers are urgently needed by the heart patients whose lives they help to save.

But Villafana has added two other important ingredients to his personal success formula. First, he goes out of his way to establish rapport with the surgeons who use his product, in order to find out exactly what qualities they require in a pacemaker. Often, in the early days, he would even go into the operating room to observe doctors implant his devices.

Second, he has concentrated on developing pacemakers with significant advantages over their competition. His original company, Cardiac Pacemakers, used longer-lasting lithium batteries while the competition was still powering their products with shorter-life mercury batteries. And his later company, St. Jude Medical, produces a smoother-working device, which he claims means that the pacemaker itself will last far longer than competitive models.

The reported results would seem to bear out his claims. At thirty-nine, a once poor Puerto Rican boy, who at times, following the death of his father, was forced to beg on the street with his mother, is now a millionaire eleven times over.

From Manuel Villafana, then, we have learned not merely to look for ways of satisfying the needs and desires of others but also to take the time and trouble to find out as exactly as possible what those needs and desires are, and then to figure out better ways of satisfying them.

In the next chapter we'll learn one of the most important success secrets of all—namely, how to operate your own research-and-development lab, whose findings won't cost you a red cent.

6

Be Your Own Research Lab

William Shakespeare's plays cover the whole spectrum of human experience. His characters range from tyrants, murderers, bullies, thieves, jealous schemers, liars, and assassins to noble kings, tender lovers, doting parents, roistering drunks, swaggering soldiers, philosophers, gravediggers, and country bumpkins.

How could one playwright, who lived all his life within a small area of England, have achieved such an encyclopedic knowledge of mankind?

The answer, of course, is by looking inside himself. In his own head and heart he found every possible trait of character and twist of emotion. His dialogue rings true because Shakespeare knew that he himself was Everyman. He had only to consult his own soul to imagine how any character would react in a given situation because he—as a human being—was also a microcosm of the whole human race.

This is something you have in common with Shakespeare.

Since each of us is a human being, each possesses within himself the whole potential range of emotions, urges, fears, anxieties, appetites, physical and emotional needs, instinctual drives, and reactions common to all.

Now, this is not just idle philosophizing. It's a fact of key importance to your own personal success story.

Major corporations such as General Motors, Du Pont, IBM, and American Tel & Tel spend hundreds of millions of dollars every year on what is called "R&D"—that is, research and development. Their labs, such as the Bell Telephone Laboratories, are like self-contained universities with vast facilities, huge staffs, expensive scientific equipment, and operating budgets large enough to run a small country.

These are the "idea hatcheries" that spew out the new products, new techniques, and new services needed to maintain their company's competitive edge against the fierce onslaught of its industrial rivals.

Obviously you, as a lone individual striving for success in a world of big business, have no way of matching such a setup. But the good news is that you don't have to.

Why? Because it just so happens that you already have the most perfect and completely equipped R&D lab ever devised for generating profitable new ideas—namely, *yourself*.

No, I'm not joking. I mean every word of that.

In Chapter 4, you'll remember, I told you that all luck starts with an idea. And, as you also know, the kinds of ideas I'm talking about relate to *people*, which, needless to say, includes *you*.

Now, these ideas (again to recap) are *problem-solving ideas*, ideas on how to *help others*, on ways to *fulfill people's needs or desires*, on how to *save people trouble or annoyance*, in short, ideas for any sort of object or service that can help to *make people's lives happier or more satisfying, comfortable, or care-free.*

When it comes to ideas in any of these categories, you—as a typical human being—make the perfect guinea pig.

For example, ask yourself right now if there is some recent nuisance or problem you've had to cope with that makes you wish someone would come up with an answer. Or is there something you'd like to be able to obtain that nobody is currently supplying?

If so, you have the germ of a money-making idea staring you right in the face. Consider the following:

- Say your car's been acting up—stalling when you stop for traffic lights or refusing to start properly when you turn on the ignition. You'd like to get it fixed pronto because you've got a long drive planned for tomorrow and would hate to get hung up far from home. But, instead, you have to phone in advance for a service appointment three days later. And on the day you do take your car in, you know darn well you'll have to wait in line for up to half an hour before the service manager gets around to looking under your hood and writing up the service order for whatever needs to be done. And you think, Gee, wouldn't it be great if I could find a mechanic who made house calls. . . . Bingo. An electric light bulb just flashed on. You've come up with an idea that could easily be developed into a profit-making venture, given the necessary input of time, effort, and capital.
- Or say you lunched in a restaurant today and ordered apple pie for dessert but what the waitress brought you was a hunk of cardboard filled with canned, chemically preserved fruit—causing you to think for the ump-

teenth time, Why can't I ever get a decent piece of homemade apple pie like Mom showed my wife how to make? . . . *Bingo.* Another electric light flashes on, and another idea for a profitable business has just taken shape. If your wife can make such good apple pie, why not have her go into production, with you peddling the pies to local restaurants and delis?

• Or say you're about to tackle a do-it-yourself home-improvement project, such as retiling the bathroom and installing a new shower enclosure. Maybe you've done some earlier work along this line, and with the help of instructional materials you're reasonably confident you can do a decent job. All the same, you'd feel a lot better if first you could get some professional advice from an experienced craftsman who could give you a few pointers that might save you considerable time, effort, and headaches. And suddenly you think, Boy, I sure wish there was some "house doctor" I could call in to diagnose the job and show me exactly how to use the tools and lay the tiles—but still leave the actual work to me. . . . *Flash.* There went the electric light blub again. You've just had an idea for a do-it-yourself home advisory service that an experienced handyman could develop into a one-man business—or that you might suggest as a sales-promotion gimmick to a local craftsmen's supply store.

In these examples I've shown you how a single brainstorming session may churn out several viable luck-making ideas. True, some of these ideas may call for more know-how, experience, or capital than you possess. But capital can be borrowed from banks or other lenders, given the right qualifications. As for experience and know-how in a given field, that's no great problem, either. You can always find people who do possess them—and, what's more, who may be eager to go in with you on a promising project. All it takes is the willingness to ask.

For instance, take that last notion—about getting a store to feature a do-it-yourself home advisory service as a sales-promotion gimmick. If you interrupt at this point to say you're no expert handyman—well, shake, brother. That makes two of us. I barely know one end of a hammer from the other.

But that wouldn't stop me.

How would I go about it? . . . Very simple. First I'd locate several competent handymen, by inquiring around or checking out the services column in the want-ad section of my local newspaper. No matter how busy they may be at the moment, most such people are only too happy to latch on to a steady additional source of income. So I'd try to arrange with them to let me act as their agent for a suitable markup. Then I'd go to the biggest supply stores in the area and explain the kind of advisory service I had in mind.

In the beginning this advisory service might be offered free by the store, during a sales week, to every customer who bought some minimum amount of do-it-yourself materials. Thereafter the service might still be offered free, to the extent of telephone consultations and question answering. An actual house call, however, would involve a moderate fee, perhaps with the store itself absorbing part of the cost as a continuing sales builder.

My role would be to supply the store with a ready-made staff of consultants, working at a set fee for each house call. The store would pay me for their services, and I in turn would pay each of the handymen after taking out my own commission.

But I'm getting ahead of myself. In later chapters I'll expand on the subject of what to do with your ideas after you get them. For the moment I'm concerned only with getting the ideas in the first place, using yourself as an ideal private R&D lab.

Not long ago I saw in the newspaper the following ad:

I CAN HELP!

Chances are you will become a victim of a burglary, vandalism, fire damage or natural disaster such as flood or wind damage. Your insurance company may not compensate you for the full amount of damage or loss unless you can prove the actual loss.

I will videotape your home inside and out, your furniture, valuables and collections. This professional-quality color tape with sound narration will verify any claim you may have to make. My videotape will provide you with a permanent record that will be virtually impossible to dispute.

The idea for this service seemed so unusual and original that I guessed at once that an electric light bulb must have flashed on in somebody's head. So I checked out the ad and, sure enough, my hunch proved correct.

The ad had been placed, I discovered, by a retired police officer who had formed his own small company to provide the service. He told me the whole story.

Two years ago, he had found himself in the hospital, faced with heavy medical bills and with only a modest pension to support himself and his family. Then, while glancing through a magazine, his attention was caught by an advertisement for videotaping equipment. He had had experience with such equipment in the course of his police work. Moreover, his duties had made him a firsthand witness of homes that had been robbed, vandalized, or damaged by disasters of various sorts. He had also seen how totally unprepared most victims are to specify and itemize their losses.

No doubt his own precarious financial position at the moment made him extra sensitive to the plight of others. At any rate, somewhere along the line, a light flashed. Putting together all the elements—the equipment ad, his police experience, and so on—he suddenly came up with a red-hot idea: Why not start up a business service offering homeowners a videotape record of their valuables?

That was two years ago. As soon as he got out of the hospital, he proceeded to act on his idea. Today he's operating a thriving business that gives him a higher income than he earned at his highest rank on the force.

And notice how, in his own special way, he used himself—with his particular experience and background—as a natural R&D lab to generate this luck-making idea.

One reason I wanted to bring in the foregoing example was by way of contrast. It so happens, you see, that I, too, came up with a luck-making idea based on much the same problem—namely, how to substantiate losses in case of a burglary, fire, or other disaster.

My solution to the problem was much different from that of the former police officer, and it was certainly prompted by much more humdrum circumstances. But here again, as in his case, the idea came about by using myself as an R&D lab or guinea pig.

One day, while out of town, I called my wife and asked her to look up a certain insurance policy. She couldn't find it—nor, like a dummy, could I tell her exactly where to look.

That experience started me thinking. Suppose there was a fire and we had to clear out of the house fast. Would I know where to lay hands on our most valuable documents in a hurry? And how well would I be able to itemize all our valuables in filing an insurance claim?

No doubt at some time or other this same question

must trouble every homeowner. But in my case, having trained myself to be especially aware of such idea-generating problems, it caused an electric light bulb to flash on in my head: Why not develop a special record book for just this purpose?

So I did. It's called Your Permanent Record Book and has places to list all your important legal and financial documents, such as insurance policies, military-service papers, stocks, bonds, etc., as well as a room-by-room record of all your household furnishings and valuables. To date I have sold over half a million copies—starting with an idea and a dummy that cost less than a hundred dollars.

Often one idea will lead to another by a sort of chain reaction. Since that's what happened in the case of Your Permanent Record Book, this is a good place to illustrate how that chain-reaction effect may occur.

I usually have a fairly busy appointment schedule, which I keep track of in the usual fashion, by means of a date book. But to my way of thinking, all such date books have a major shortcoming. For some reason or other they show only a single week at a time—which is seldom the way my schedule (or, I suspect, the schedule of any other businessman) gets laid out. As a result, I would constantly find myself flipping back and forth from one page of my datebook to another.

Although I'd been vaguely aware of this problem from time to time, it was something merely flickering on the fringes of my consciousness—and ordinarily it might have remained there. The problem didn't loom large enough to stir me into figuring out a solution.

But I'd just recently designed Your Permanent Record Book and maybe that inclined me to take a more critical look at the subject. If I could figure out a useful and profitable record book to help a homemaker keep track of his valuables, why couldn't I figure out a more sensible and convenient date book for businessmen?

Okay, I thought, let's give it a whirl. The problem is how to design a date book that will give the businessman-user a broader overview of his schedule at a single glance. And even as I stated the problem to myself in this way, that old electric light bulb flashed and a simple solution sprang to mind: Why not design a date book with a whole week of days on each facing page; so anytime the user opens the book he can see two weeks of his schedule, side by side?

Once this answer occurred to me, it seemed so obvious that it was hard to believe that no one had come up with such a date book long ago. But as it turned out, to the best of my knowledge, I had the field all to myself.

Once again, I produced the book and had it merchandised by mail order. Its advantages were obvious at a glance to any businessman who saw it. Orders came pouring in.

As always, this piece of "luck" involved no stroke of genius on my part—just an idea so simple anyone could have thought of it. But apparently no one had. Either I was the only one who did think of it or the only one who did anything about it. Result: The profit was all mine.

And the chain reaction didn't end there.

I have a brother-in-law who's one of the world's sweetest guys. I'm fond of him, and he reciprocates my regard. But one day, while we were chatting on the phone, his manner seemed a mite cool and withdrawn. I sensed that something had gotten under his skin.

We've always been able to talk frankly to each other, so I asked him what was wrong. After a bit of verbal fencing he finally admitted to being peeved. Why? Because *he* always remembered *my* wedding anniversary with a card, whereas I rarely remembered *his*. And I'd just forgotten again.

Well, I uttered appropriate soothing noises, and he signed off somewhat mollified. But I hung up feeling thoroughly annoyed with myself. His anniversary wasn't the only date I goofed on. The truth is, I'm constantly guilty of failing to remember people's birthdays and other such occasions.

Right then and there I vowed that *next* year I'd do better. I'd remember all the dates important to my family and friends with cards, phone calls, gifts, or letters.

At least that's what I resolved in the mood of the moment.

But I wondered how well I'd keep my resolution. Just looking up and entering all those dates on the calendar would amount to quite a chore in itself. And by the time next year's calendar came out I might well have forgotten the whole thing.

What I had here, in other words, was a *problem,* and one that was no doubt common to thousands of other people.

If I could come up with a solution, I thought, I might well have a real luck-maker. . . . Hmm.

Suddenly an electric light bulb flashed on in my mind: Human beings may have faulty memories, but computers don't. Why not program a computer to crank out the individual reminder schedules I'd need to offer such a service to the public?

Easier said than done, unfortunately. I had already made up my mind to use the same basic format as I'd used in my two-weeks-at-a-glance date book. The weeks would be printed without dates, merely showing the names of the days, starting with Sunday. This would enable the computer to print out the reminder dates, and the diary could start at any time of the year rather than on the usual January 1.

The major hitch turned out to be finding a way for the computer printout to be made on both sides of a page. But this problem, too, was finally solved.

I called the result a "computerized diary." Everyone I showed it to thought it was a terrific idea and would sell like hotcakes. In no time I arranged to have the product merchandised by mail order, just as the date book and record book were.

Alas, this time my great idea didn't pan out. Sales lagged. And eventually I discovered why. The merchandising organizations I'd chosen were aimed at middle-class America, whereas the product's appeal was primarily to wealthier, upper-class buyers. Now I've been offered a deal with one of America's most exclusive companies to market a much snazzier version, and once again the profit picture looks very bright.

Which, incidentally, brings up another important rule of thumb: Never discard an idea till you've checked out its potential from every possible angle. (We will explore this more in Chapter 7.)

Notice once again that each of the three ideas I've just described was generated by my own R&D lab, based on a problem encountered in my own personal experience: forgetting a relative's anniversary; wanting a date book that would enable me to see more than one week at a glance; my wife being unable to lay hands on a certain insurance policy.

That retired police officer I mentioned was concerned with a somewhat similar problem—namely, a verifiable record of a homeowner's valuables—but his solution to the problem evolved in a totally different direction from mine.

Now, so far I've emphasized the idea of you as a typical human being, a universal guinea pig, a microcosm of the whole human race—and therefore that *your* wants, needs, and problems are likely to be shared by millions of other people. But the same guinea-pig notion holds true in more specialized cases as well, such as for members of a certain ethnic group, residents of a given locale, males or females only, or members of a given profession.

For instance, there's a hive of professional cartoonists who live in one part of Connecticut, and every week they have to deliver artwork to newspaper syndicates in New York City, especially to one particular syndicate. As you might expect, someone got the bright idea of setting up a weekly delivery service just for that one small group of customers—and made it pay.

On a larger scale, you may recall how a couple of years ago, as our country's postal service deteriorated, individuals in various towns or cities began to set up their own private, local mail service with guaranteeed same-day delivery. The government eventually put them out of business on purely legal grounds, but before that happened, all of them were prospering. Why? Because in every case the individual who started the service had checked his private R&D lab and discovered from personal experience that the mails were becoming slow and unreliable—and therefore realized that the public would eagerly go for something better.

In the previous chapter I told how two young attorneys in New York City came to specialize in serving one particular type of client, as a result of their personal experience when they took on the first such case as a favor. Their clientele is now limited to illegal aliens, but by serving the needs of that one group, they have built up a thriving practice.

Ruth Grosstetter, you'll recall, built up a profitable spare-time activity catering to local housewives like herself who appreciated the services of a manicurist willing to come to their own homes at convenient times.

Another woman, Ruth Handler, with the same first name but a much more specialized problem resulting from her mastectomy, is now running a large national corporation whose business consists of supplying artificial breasts to women with the same need as herself. It would be hard to find a more dramatic illustration of an individual marketing a highly successful product generated by her own private R&D lab.

Almost anywhere you look, you'll find products or services that were sparked in just that same way—by someone whose *personal need* inspired him to go into business fulfilling that same need for other people.

In your own home, for instance, you may have a telephone stand or phone pad with a pencil attached to it by a chain. How do you suppose that product originated? . . . Foolish question. Obviously some person repeatedly had to look around for a pencil to jot something down when he answered the phone, but could never find one when he needed it.

And, presto, an electric light bulb suddenly lit up in his head: How about a pencil attached to the phone stand by a chain? And no doubt at the same moment he instantly realized that thousands of other people would be willing to shell out money for that same simple product.

On a recent trip to Japan I was startled to see the brand-new answer to a problem that first occurred to me years ago. I remember sitting in a restaurant and, while ordering lunch, I asked the waiter about a certain item on the menu. He gave me his offhand opinion of the dish, which told me little or nothing. What I really wanted was a chance to *see* the dish, so I could judge for myself just how appetizing or unappetizing it looked.

Over the years, that same thought flashed through my mind many times—especially at restaurants specializing in some foreign cuisine: If only I could get a look at the dish before I order it. I was convinced that if restaurants would respond to this desire, they could greatly increase their business—because whenever customers are uncertain about what they'll get, they tend to be timid about ordering.

In time, of course, various restaurant chains offering a standardized choice of foods began to feature pictures of the dishes on their menu. This was certainly a step in the right direction, but never seemed to me a completely satisfactory answer.

Well, let me tell you, on that trip to Japan I saw what has to be the slickest answer to date. In front of almost every restaurant in Tokyo you'll see all the items on the menu publicly displayed—*in plastic,* yet so realistic-looking you'd almost swear they just came out of the kitchen.

I was told that all these food displays are manufactured by one firm or individual who holds a patent on the process. And I'd be willing to bet my wallet that the idea first occurred to this unsung genius the same way it occurred to me—while hesitantly ordering a meal in a restaurant and wondering what some item on the menu looked like.

Actually, examples are endless of people using themselves as R&D labs to generate successful ideas.

The Pepperidge Farm baking business began because a woman had the knack of making delicious, old-fashioned home-baked bread for her own family, and knew that other people would be glad to buy such bread if it were available.

The Gerber baby-food business began because a young couple, aware of the time and trouble it took to cook, strain, and process food for their own infants, reasoned correctly that other parents would be willing to pay to have such food prepared for *their* babies.

In the same way, by being on the lookout at all times, morning to night, for products or services that *you* would like to see offered, you'll also be turning up ideas that can be widely marketed to other people.

HOMEWORK

Get pencil and paper and do exactly as I suggested earlier in this chapter. Draw up a list of common wants or needs that *you* would like to see conveniently fulfilled for your own sake. Then, for each of these wants or needs, try to figure out a way of servicing that need for a large number of people. Remember: Each such answer you come up with is the potential nucleus of a successful money-making business.

7

Take Off Those Blinkers

*B*linkers, or blinders, are put on a horse's bridle for a good reason—to keep the horse from seeing things on either side that might make him skittish.

Offhand I can't think of any good reason why a human being would want to wear blinkers. True, there are times when it pays to concentrate on a set goal and not let yourself be distracted by side issues or diversions. But in terms of your career you'll generally find it pays to keep a well-rounded view at all times.

Can you imagine trying to drive a car without being able to see pedestrians or other vehicles approaching on your right or left? Every cross street you pass would become an invitation to disaster.

A horse wearing blinkers has a driver at the reins to guide him in the proper direction. But you, as a self-starter charting your own career course, need a constant input of facts, perceptions, and ideas flowing into your awareness from all quarters if you hope to compete successfully in the world around you.

This isn't just a matter of prudence—it's a matter of *creative luck making.*

Let me give you the most dramatic single illustration I can think of: During World War II hundreds of thousands of young landlubbers had to be trained and shipped out to sea quickly for service in the Navy and Coast Guard, with no time to develop their sea legs. Needless to say, many suffered terrible bouts of seasickness, which rendered them temporarily unfit to carry out their shipboard duties.

A drug was urgently needed to combat the malady, and scientists soon came up with an answer. The curative agent they developed proved quite effective, save for one unfortunate side effect—it tended to cause drowsiness. Still, this was a minor drawback compared to the original problem of seasickness. As a result, the drug was put into large-scale production.

Peacetime, however, brought a totally different problem to the drug's manufacturer. With no more mass induction of naval recruits, who would buy the stuff? People might go on getting seasick or motion sick, but overnight the market for the drug had shrunk to the vanishing point. For a while it looked as though that division of the company might fail.

Then an electric light bulb flashed in somebody's mind. That "somebody" had a brilliant but simple idea—which may already have occurred to *you* as you read this.

Why not capitalize on the drowsiness-inducing aspect of the product and sell it to nerve-frazzled people looking for a good night's rest? In other words, forget that the drug company was peddling a seasickness cure. Take what had previously been downplayed as an unfortunate side effect and sell *that* to the public instead. Today that product is one of the leading over-the-counter sleep-inducing products.

This is another way of saying, *take off your blinkers* and try looking at the problem from a fresh point of view.

Pitched in a new way to new buyers, your product or service may have a vastly greater sales appeal than you ever imagined.

By the same token, your luck-making ideas may have a vastly greater potential if you will keep turning them over and over in your mind, looking for a new angle—or a new answer to some popular need.

Jean Nidetch, of Great Neck, New York, was an overweight housewife who, like millions of other Americans, male and female, wanted to thin down. But—again like millions of other Americans—she wasn't having too much luck with her dieting. She noticed that she seemed to get better results just from talking over her reducing problems with friends who were in the same boat.

Somewhere along the line, an electric light bulb lit up in her head. Alcoholics Anonymous had proved that drinkers could cope more successfully with their drinking problem if they shared in the combined strength of others involved in the same battle. Gamblers Anonymous did a similar job for compulsive gamblers. Why not apply the same approach to people with a weight problem?

Jean Nidetch began by organizing a circle of overweight women who met weekly in one another's homes to be weighed before an audience of their peers and to share sympathetically in the shame and embarrassment of backsliding or to bask in the triumphant glow of having shed another pound or two. Through lively discussion, the exchange of tips and suggestions, and the goading of group criticism, confirmed fatties actually found themselves losing weight for the first time.

So successful did her strategy prove that Jean Nidetch founded a nationwide organization called Weight Watchers Anonymous to set up similar groups all over the country. In time she found herself running such a thriving business that her organization was purchased by the Heinz Company.

Today Jean Nidetch is a multimillionaire—all because she removed her one-solution blinkers, took a fresh look at the problem of losing weight, and found that better results could be obtained by concentrating on group support rather than on diet alone.

Mental blinkers can narrow our marketing vision in a number of surprising ways. I recall reading about a young woman named Doris G. She had a good accounting background, but the résumés she kept sending out had uniformly negative results. She found one unsuccessful application particularly depressing because she had thought herself ideally suited to the job.

Finally she took her problem to an employment counselor. He read her letter and résumé, then asked, "How many people do you suppose applied for that job?"

Doris was able to answer exactly—"Fifty-six"—because she had a friend who worked for the company that had advertised the position.

"Well, now," the counselor went on, "your qualifications as outlined in your letter and résumé seem quite adequate, but how many of those other fifty-six applicants also had adequate qualifications?"

Doris shurgged glumly. "Most of them, I suppose."

"Probably so," the counselor agreed. "Then why would you expect the department manager of that company to pick you over any of the other applicants?"

Doris couldn't answer the question because it had never occurred to her.

"You see," the counselor pointed out, "what your letter *should* have done was not just indicate to the prospective employer that you're well suited to the job. It should have persuaded him that you're *better* suited than any of the competition."

On her next application Doris did just that. She took the trouble to find out in advance just what the job opening involved. Then she gave the matter some creative thought, trying to figure out what special skills or experience or ideas she could bring to bear on such a bookkeeping position that might enable her to do a better job for the prospective employer than the next applicant whose letter he opened.

This time her letter resulted in a phone call, an interview, and a job offer—all because she had taken off her blinkers and looked at the problem from the employer's point of view rather than from her own as a job seeker.

How many times have you gone into a clothing store and dealt with a salesperson who tries to sell you, not the sort of suit or dress *you* are looking for, but the kind he or she thinks you should have. When that happens to me, I'm afraid I lose patience fast. If I can't get the nagging salesman off my back, I simply go elsewhere.

I've encountered a new-car salesman in an automobile dealership who stubbornly insisted on trying to sell me a model he had on the floor, rather than listen to what I wanted and offer to get it for me. No doubt he had been ordered by his boss to push that particular model, and there was certainly no harm in trying. But to keep on trying to unload it despite my clear and obvious negative signals was simply self-defeating. He didn't sell me that floor model— nor did he get my order.

The next place I went didn't have the precise color and model in stock that I wanted, either. But *this* salesman offered to try to get it for me immediately by arranging a trade with some other dealership in the vicinity. In twenty-four hours he had me behind the wheel of the car I wanted, and he also had a deal—simply because he didn't handicap himself with blinkers or earplugs.

* * *

In the days when Israel was struggling for nationhood and the right of Jews everywhere to immigrate to their historic homeland, British opposition to these aspirations aroused widespread resentment among American Jews. Rabbi Stephen S. Wise organized a boycott of all British products.

Lipton Tea, though actually owned by a Dutch firm, Lever Brothers Company, was widely assumed to be English, thanks to the familiar image of its founder, the famed British merchant and yacht-racing enthusiast, Commodore Thomas Lipton. In consequence, it suffered heavily from the Jewish boycott.

Robert Smallwood, then head of Lipton, went to plead his case to Rabbi Wise, who sympathized with him over the injustice of the situation but could offer no solution as long as the boycott continued.

Someone, however, suggested to Smallwood that I, as a public-relations counselor, might be able to help him with his problem. When he came to me, the answer seemed so obvious that I was able to provide it on the spot and thereby earned a sizable fee.

I suggested that Lipton commission the famed artist Arthur Szyk—who was my client—to do a beautifully illuminated text, suitable for framing, of Israel's Declaration of Independence. I advised that Lipton then take ads in various Jewish publications offering a copy of Szyk's work for fifty cents and two Lipton tea box tops.

Not only did the ads pay for themselves; in a short time Lipton had completely reversed its image in the eyes of American Jews.

The answer to Lipton's problem was simple, but it became apparent only when Smallwood removed his blinkers—or, rather, *had* them removed. Initially he had seen the problem as a need to persuade American Jews that Lipton was a Dutch firm, not English.

Instead, by offering them enticing and visible proof of his sympathy for Israel, he caused them to draw their conclusions—swiftly and automatically.

Notice that the blinker concept may apply to the *problem* or to the *solution*—or to both.

For example, when they were still new to the field, the people who make Osterizer blenders were desperately seeking a way to increase sales. But the Waring blender seemed to have a corner on the market. So Osterizer asked me to come up with a solution.

I noticed that most of their sales brochures and instruction booklets had to do with the use of mixers in bars, and dealt only briefly with the use of mixers in home kitchens. This seemed strange, since there are hundreds of thousands more home kitchens than there are public bars. Why expend so much time and effort going after a small segment of the market—especially a segment that a competitor already has sewn up—when a much larger market is waiting to be exploited?

When I pointed out this obvious fact, they altered their whole marketing approach and sales zoomed.

In this case you might say that Osterizer was trying to solve the wrong problem (that is, how to sell more mixers to bars), whereas Lipton was concentrating on the wrong solution.

This is often a fruitful perspective from which to analyze and improve your own luck-making ideas.

For instance, say you want to get a raise from your boss. Instead of looking for impressive new facts and figures on inflation and the spiraling cost of living with which to convince him a raise is in order, maybe a better way is to come up with some fresh new ideas for improving the business or upping the efficiency of your department— then let him decide for himself that you deserve a raise.

Or suppose you want to be better liked by your circle of acquaintances or the people you work with. Instead of dreaming up clever ploys to influence their opinion of you, why not try changing yourself into a better person?

Or take the case of New York City's pushcart peddlers. In the recession of 1980 it seemed to many that their best market strategy would be to offer even lower-priced goods to their traditional customers on the Lower East Side, among the city's less affluent economic stratum.

But the peddlers chose a different, more successful strategy. They offered better-quality merchandise to a whole new class of customers higher up on the socioeconomic scale. As a result, they can now be seen hawking items such as perfume, leather goods, and even designer garments on uptown street corners in competition with Manhattan's best department stores.

In other words, instead of pulling in their horns and concentrating on serving a narrow segment of the market more intensively, they've actually expanded their market by seeking out a whole new class of customers—namely, well-to-do uptowners, who now, for the first time, are showing an eagerness to shop on the street for goods at cut-rate prices.

Still another way of removing blinkers is to look at the goods or services you wish to offer the public in a brand-new light, and with a critical eye that takes nothing for granted.

For example, the sport of tossing a Frisbee first began at a baking company that bore the name of Frisbie. During lunch hour the employees liked to gather outdoors behind the plant and toss back and forth the plastic pie plates that the company used in packaging its products.

As the fad began to spread to other parts of the country, an electric light bulb suddenly flashed on in the heads of management. Instead of making pies and cakes, they went out of the baking business altogether and began to manufacture plastic Frisbees.

A woman in our community with whom my wife is acquainted began to baby-sit as a spare-time way of picking up extra money. But the field was crowded, especially on afternoons and evenings, by high-school girls who undercut her hourly price.

As she cast about for additional employment it suddenly struck her that she had been overlooking a whole unserved group of clients—namely, those who had elderly relatives in their household to care for. Often these elderly individuals needed escorts to take them on walks or, if confined to a wheelchair, needed someone to wheel them on brief outings, or simply needed companionship at home when other members of the family were away. If ailing as well as aged, they might need someone on hand in case of emergency—not necessarily an expensive trained nurse, but someone who could summon help when needed.

By advertising her services as a sitter for elderly people, the woman now finds herself swamped with business.

An interesting twist on this has recently been reported from West Germany, where an enterprising young lady has founded a "rent-a-grandma" baby-sitting service. After reading that the municipal government in Paris sponsors and subsidizes a service by which elderly women, mostly widows, baby-sit *free of charge,* Beate Kramer decided to try out the same idea in Hamburg.

She put an ad in the local paper, asking elderly women to write her if they liked children and were willing to look after them without pay. The response surprised her. A number of women, including retired teachers and nurses who were bored doing nothing, said they would be happy to take on such assignments. Beate now has 130 grandmas to rent and *pays them* a small fee after taking her own commission as organizer and operator of the service.

An even more stunning example is the toy called Slinky, that spiral coil able to flop its own way downstairs, step by step. It began as a machine part on a ship. Richard James was working for the Navy on a test run when a torsion spring fell off and bounced on the floor. He was amused with the bouncing spring and thought it could be made into a toy. He later developed Slinky, the famous toy. Today, decades later, Slinky is a staple of the toy industry.

But wait'll you hear this. Can you imagine someone bottling and selling tap water? Believe it or not, it's being done. New York City tap water is bottled there, then sold in California to expatriate New Yorkers addicted to the taste of their own native tipple, who just can't get used to the West Coast stuff.

If you've thought about starting up a lawn service but find the field overcrowded with franchise operators and professional landscape gardeners, maybe the answer is to dream up a new angle and specialize. A high-schooler I know specializes (expertly, I might add) in weed killing for people whose lawns are invaded by stubborn crabgrass and other nuisances. There's also a woman, whose ads I've seen in our local newspaper, who will come to your house and design, plant, and tend a flower garden especially to your taste.

There's also a teenage rock group that is offered a lot of gigs to play at parties, especially birthday parties, not only in their own community but in surrounding towns as well—and guess how. As a unique feature (and for an extra fee, of course) they will compose and play a song named after the host or hostess or guest of honor. Whenever they are hired to play at a birthday party, this special service is nearly always requested.

Speaking of parties, did you know there are women who specialize in staging parties for children? And not only kiddy parties, but birthday and sweet-sixteen parties. They cater the refreshments, provide the decorations and favors, book the entertainment, and program the games or other activities needed to make the party go.

And do you know how a good many of these party specialists have built up their reputations and clientele? Their unique careers hinge most of all on their originality in creating theme parties—such as "hard times" parties, "fairy tale" parties, "treasure-hunting" parties, "who-dun-it" parties, and so on. In other words, they have established businesses by injecting pizzazz into an old and often hackneyed fun-time activity.

The secret, you might say, is not to reinvent old things but to take off your blinkers and "see" new ways of presenting those old things to the public.

Early in the century, for instance, a druggist in New Jersey noticed how often people would come into his store to buy a roll of gauze and of adhesive tape when all they really wanted was a bandage. So he began cutting out pieces of gauze and tape and preparing ready-made bandages for his customers. This service grew so popular that he gradually realized he had invented a whole new product—and that's how Band-Aids were born.

A perceptive couple named DeWitt and Lila Wallace, of Pleasantville, New York, took a keen look at the magazine field in the 1920s and realized how many different magazines an individual would have to read in order to keep up with all the interesting and useful new information being reported each month.

Taking this thought a step further, they began cutting up magazines on the kitchen table and assembling models of a brand-new publication that would do just that—namely, give the reader a concise digest, under one cover, of all the interesting and useful information gleaned from a whole range of popular magazines. The result was *Reader's Digest*, which became the nucleus of a giant publishing empire.

Three decades later, the television industry had taken shape and was expanding at a breathless pace. Each day's network programming was listed in the daily newspapers, just as radio programming had always been listed. But a shrewd publisher named Walter H. Annenberg took off his blinkers and viewed the subject from a brand-new angle.

Television was then in its exciting, youthful "Golden Age." It was offering the public richer, more varied fare than had come to them over radio, and to many families whose TV sets were a recent acquisition, the programming was still new and unfamiliar. Television, moreover, played to both the eye and the ear, and therefore, unlike radio, demanded the audience's full attention. As a result, people became so involved in and addicted to the medium that they were constantly leafing through the paper to the entertainment section to see what was being offered on the various channels.

Annenberg got the revolutionary idea that the public would be willing to pay money for a small, handy magazine that offered nothing but a description of the networks' programming schedules. Some considered the idea ridiculous, but events proved him right. Viewers soon came to consider his brainchild an essential aid to television viewing. Today *TV Guide* has the largest circulation of any magazine and is also the single most profitable publication in the magazine racks.

Still another unblinkered look at the publishing industry was taken by a man named Harry Scherman, who got the notion that many people might be hesitant about buying books simply because they were unsure what books were *worth* buying. Ergo, why not form a committee of several erudite experts to advise the public on this subject by choosing the best books published each month—and then sign up subscribers who would agree in advance to buy a certain number of the committee's monthly selections?

The result was the immensely profitable Book-of-the-Month Club, which not only established a whole new marketing channel for the industry outside of regular bookstores but also turned most of its newly tapped buyers into dependable repeat customers, thereby greatly reducing the sales expense.

George Macy had an equally hot marketing idea—this one aimed at a more exclusive, higher-income group of buyers. He put out beautifully bound and illustrated editions of world-famous classics—books of universal appeal—and to add to their snob value had only a limited number printed, each one signed by the artist. These, sold through the Limited Editions Book Club, were followed up with a larger printing of unsigned and somewhat less expensively bound but still beautifully designed books, and sold to a wider group of subscribers under the imprint of the Heritage Book Club.

In other words, he not only devised a new type of book for a special market, but in publishing each such book, he regularly exploited that market in two successive, money-making ways.

Notice how each of these success stories involved finding a *new angle* or a *new slant* on an already existing commodity or service—and tapped a new vein of profit. The exciting, fascinating annals of American business are full of such triumphant examples.

Back in the days when all car seats were upholstered in plush, stains were hard to remove. This gave Manny Fingerhut, of Minneapolis, the idea that a good many buyers might be willing to invest in ready-made seat covers to protect their new car's upholstery. There was no way to tailor the product precisely to fit a particular car, but at that time the range of models and interior dimensions was sufficiently limited so that a few sizes would provide at least an approximate fit for most cars.

As always, there were plenty of scoffers. But Manny Fingerhut had taken off the blinkers and therefore could see the buyer's viewpoint as well as his own. He canvassed dealerships in his area for the names of new-car buyers, then solicited each one by direct mail. The business was successful from the start. It grew so fast that eventually his mailing lists were taken from the new-car registrations in every state. His company became a plum that was finally absorbed by a large conglomerate, and now does an annual *three-hundred-million-dollar* business—all because Manny Fingerhut looked at the car seat-cover market from a new and original point of view.

Diners Club was started when businessman Frank McNamara, Ralph Snyder, a lawyer, and Alfred Bloomingdale had dinner in Majors Cabin Grill, near the Empire State Building. Frank McNamara, who owned a company called Hamilton Credit Corporation, told of a Bronx man who owed him two thousand dollars and from whom he was having trouble collecting. It seems that this man would let local people charge in the drugstore and other neighborhood stores on his account, then they would pay him back with interest. The locals using this man's charge account bought not only drugs but also other things, and ran up big bills.

Snyder and Bloomingdale both realized at that moment that there was a need for individuals who have no charge privileges to use someone else's charge account and be willing to pay for it. Snyder and Bloomingdale bought out the Hamilton Credit Corporation and created the Diners Club.

On a similar scale, but from an equally creative impulse, two women in Tenafly, New Jersey—Harriet Greenwald and Fern Gallant—took a keen new look at the travel business. What about men and women who had only a day off from work and had nothing exciting or unusual to look forward to on that day, yet were as avid for recreation and diversion as any other tourist-agency customer? Their idea was to organize tours and outings that would take their patrons no farther than a half hour's ride from town. You think the scope of their idea is too small? Not so: It's already a thriving business, and they're considering franchising the concept.

Even professional men such as lawyers and accountants can come up with brand-new ideas for expanding their practices if they take off the blinkers for a fresh look. I've already told you about the two attorneys who found themselves an eager horde of new clients simply by their willingness to tackle the thorny problems facing illegal aliens. Another, even more profitable specialty that has zoomed to importance just in the last decade or so is representing actors and athletes. Actors had often employed agents, but less often retained their own lawyers and accountants; athletes had rarely been represented in any of these ways. Both groups have now entered the realm of big business, thereby opening a whole new field of opportunity for such legal and business reps.

One final example from my own experience: As public-relations counselor to the West German government I was called on to advise the makers of Hummel porcelain figurines while they were introducing their figurines in the U.S. market. These figurines, if not fine art, nevertheless embody craftsmanship of a high order; the product is often called the poor man's Meissen. Hummel's output included 150 designs, making theirs one of the largest lines of porcelain in the world.

Their products might have sold well when first introduced, but I thought they might also suffer an early falling off in sales as the fad or initial public enthusiasm for Hummel's figurines waned.

To avoid this, I suggested emphasizing the collectibles aspect by sharply limiting the number of models chosen for export and also by keeping some sets purposely incomplete or in short supply. Thus, the collector is not merely buying a lovely piece of porcelain; he's also investing in a "limited edition" whose beauty and value is enhanced by its scarcity.

In other words, we took the blinkers off the buyer, causing *him* to perceive the product in a very special way, which made it more profitable and advantageous to us, the seller.

How well this strategy has worked is shown by the fact that Hummel figurines remain in keen demand year after year, setting an example that other producers, such as the Franklin Mint, have sought to emulate. Indeed, Hummel early on helped set the stage for the continuing, trendy phenomenon of collectibles.

In summary, when working on *luck-making ideas*, scrutinize every lead, every thought starter, every initial inspiration, with the following questions in mind:

- Is there *another way* to tackle this problem?
- Is there a *better way* to serve this need?
- Could the product I'm working on be put to an altogether *different use?*
- Is there any *new, untapped market* for this product or service?
- *Who* might have some *new, offbeat use* for this product or service?
- How can the public be made to *perceive* this product in a startlingly *new, more impressive light?*
- Can the product or service be *introduced* or *offered* to the public in some brand-new way?

- *Whose aid* can be enlisted to help *promote* this product or service?
- *What facts* about this product, service, or need have I so far *overlooked, neglected,* or *ignored?*
- What possible *new outlets* exist for selling or distributing this product or service?

Needless to say, these questions are only a few of the ways in which you should sniff, examine, and walk around your problem in order to study it from every angle.

The Chinese call *luck* opportunity, and they say that opportunity knocks every day at your door. Some people hear it and some people do not. Some people let opportunity come into their house; some people keep opportunity waiting. Once opportunity is in the door, some people know how to accept it; others just let him stand and wait. It's not enough to hear opportunity knock. You must let him in, greet him, make friends, and work together.

8

My Million-Dollar Secret

*T*en years ago, I first met the man I will call Tom Hoffman. He was then twenty-eight, in market research at an advertising agency. He came on as a real eager beaver, full of ambitious plans for the future. Eventually he wanted to start his own business.

I've known Ed Riebling about half as long as I've known Tom. Ed, too, was in his late twenties when we first met—a printing-firm salesman, as ambitious and gung-ho as Tom. They make as neat and dramatic a comparison as I can think of.

Today, Tom Hoffman works for a different ad agency, but otherwise things haven't changed much for him. Although he's making more money, most of the increase is eaten up by inflation. He no longer talks about starting his own business—in fact there's no sign he's even likely to be promoted to head of his own department in the foreseeable future. Somehow he gives the impression of a guy who has sunk into a rut from which he'll never emerge.

Tom's manner has subtly changed, too. He seems a

mite cynical and bitter as he approaches middle age, maybe a little too inclined to blame others when anything goes wrong. From time to time, no doubt, he still daydreams of success, but his remarks along that line are too vague and pie-in-the-skyish to be taken seriously. Whatever hopes he may cherish of someday making it big, you sense it'll never happen.

With Ed Riebling it's a different story. He's no longer in the printing business. He now heads up his own sales-training firm, with a highly profitable line of instructional films and tapes that he produces himself. He conducts training seminars for major corporations all over the country, writes a column for a business magazine, dabbles in real estate, and sells products by mail order. In five years he's gone an impressive way toward making his first million.

Tom Hoffman versus Ed Riebling. One stuck in a rut, the other fireballing his way to success.

Yet both started out with more or less equal intelligence, education, enthusiasm, ability to generate promising new ideas—in short, with very nearly equal prospects.

What made the difference? How did Ed get so lucky, whereas Tom can't seem to get off dead center?

Ah, there we come to the very mainspring of this whole business of making your own luck.

I call it my *million-dollar secret*—yet you can have it for the price of this book.

In this one simple step you have the essence of all successful career building or money making or just plain friend making, whatever it is you're seeking in life.

Without it, I can say flatly you'll never get to first base. With it, you're on your way.

So what is this great secret?

Let's review for a moment. We've learned that all luck

starts with an *idea.* You can get these ideas by developing a constant *awareness*—by keeping your eyes and ears and mind open at all times and observing what goes on around you.

You notice that people have needs and desires and problems that clamor for a solution. What's more, you have a private research lab—yourself—to check out all such data personally.

Sooner or later an electric light bulb will flash on in your head as you think of a better, quicker, or more convenient way to satisfy those needs or desires or to answer those problems. Remember that people are ready to *reward* you for helping them out in this way.

So, okay, now you have your great idea. Next question: How are you going to execute it or carry it out?

The answer is by *making a connection.*

To illustrate, let me give you an example, one that comes instantly to mind because it happened to me recently.

In these days of heavy inflation and fixed incomes, money problems are universal. Whenever the subject comes up in conversation, everyone seems to agree on the urgent need to live within a budget.

Yet when you ask these same people if they themselves do so, almost invariably they tell you they've tried to work one out but can't.

Needless to say, as soon as this fact impressed itself on my mind, that famous electric light bulb flashed. Could be I had a luck-making idea here.

So I gave the matter some thought. The principles of formulating a budget are simple enough. Basically, if you can predict your approximate income, then subtract your fixed expenses, such as utilities, taxes, rent or mortgage payments, and the like, based on last year's experience, the difference will be the amount of money at your disposal for day-to-day living. Of course if your income goes up or down monthly, you may feel free to live it up a bit or to trim the fat accordingly.

Obviously, the main problem is getting the right figures together and then working your way systematically through the underbrush. I could already see in my mind's eye a simple workbook that would guide the reader, step by step, through the necessary arithmetic.

Hmm, sounded good so far, but then what? Once I get my simplified budget maker doped out, what do I do with it?

As I turned the question over in my mind, banks seemed a logical starting point. After all, money and banks have a natural association in most people's thinking.

So I flipped through my mental card file and phoned a friend who works for a company that supplies premiums to banks—that is, the gifts or prizes banks offer to depositors who open a new account.

Would any bank be interested, I inquired, in a gadget to help customers live within a budget?

"What do you have in mind?" he asked. When I started to explain, he suddenly interrupted: "Wait a minute. There's someone else I want to hear this."

The upshot was that they asked to see my budget maker as soon as I had a dummy workbook made up to show them. "There's one bank I'm sure would take five thousand right away," my friend told me, "and we do business with forty banks."

Bang. In one phone call I had *made a connection.*

And as if to bear out the old saying that it never rains but it pours, I received a phone call that same afternoon from another friend, who had just been elected board chairman of a financial institution that has to do with insurance companies. He, too, wanted to hear about my budget-maker idea, and we made a lunch appointment for the following week.

Thus, in the space of a few hours, I had made a second connection.

True, not everyone has friends so conveniently placed that they can provide instant marketing channels for your latest bright idea. This is something that comes from years of making your own luck, and it's an important aspect that I'll go into later in more detail.

For the moment I want to make clear what I mean by a connection.

Mind you, the connection may not always be to someone who can directly help you market your product or service. There are any number of more roundabout ways in which you may choose to go, or may *have* to go, in order to turn your idea into a reality.

For instance, you might contact a friend who possesses some item of equipment, such as a roto-tiller or a pickup truck, which you would need in order to perform your particular service or develop your product. You might contact a potential customer in order to check out your idea and see whether or not he would go for it. You might consult a friend with some specialized know-how or expertise relevant to your idea, in order to pick his brains. We'll go into some of these aspects in just a moment.

What matters is the *contact* itself—the getting in touch with someone who, in some way, big or small, can help you achieve the goal you're setting out to accomplish.

It's almost as if by doing so, you're calling for an electric spark—making it leap out to propel your project into motion.

Think of all those old Frankenstein movies in which the mad scientist throws a switch, causing a tremendous bolt of electricity to arc across his laboratory electrodes—

and slowly but surely the giant body on the slab starts to stir into life.

In exactly the same way—by making a connection—you will be making your idea come to life.

That person-to-person flow of energy is the magic ingredient that turns your abstract idea into an actual, on-going process. Equally important is the fact that making a connection represents a form of *action* on your part, so that it also helps to stir *you* into life and gets you going on your luck-making project.

That's why I call making a connection my million-dollar secret. Every time you contact a person you are making another connection.

Let's turn back to our opening example. Ed Riebling started making connections at an early state of his career, and kept on making connections, thereby turning his ideas into reality and parlaying them into an ever-expanding business empire.

Tom, on the other hand, never has gotten around to making any connections as far as his bright ideas for achieving success are concerned. He used to talk about them a lot in the early days of our acquaintance, but unfortunately that's all he ever did do.

This, incidentally, is a danger always to be guarded against—too much talking. Ask any professional writer and he'll tell you that the book or story that gets talked about too much is a book or story that will never get written. It's as if by talking, the author uses up the creative energy that he needs to get the story down on paper.

By the same token, excessive gab can waste the driving energy that *you* need to develop your career ideas into successful business ventures. Instead of fueling your engine of success, all that conversational energy simply heats up the atmosphere around you, turning your wonderful ideas into mere hot air.

Talk, by all means—but use your talk to make a connection.

At this point you may object that the concept of making a connection is too vague, too general. What sort of connection? you may ask—and with whom?

Those questions can be answered specifically only in terms of a given project. The possible variations are endless, but the following examples may indicate more concretely what I mean:

- You make a connection with a firsthand source of *information* about an area you wish to explore commercially.

   Example: When I first became interested in computerizing astrology, I needed to know who the top astrologers were. After a couple of hours in the library I had a list of those most quoted and interviewed. I spent months traveling to various countries in order to talk to the world's most famous astrologers and to assess their work and get an overall view of the field. The connections I made not only provided me with the information I needed but also helped to fire my enthusiasm for the subject.

- You make a connection with someone possessing the *expertise* needed to develop your product or service.

   Example: Having decided that computerized astrology was commercially feasible, I hired the most gifted astrologer I could find, as well as a top computer expert, and then worked with both to develop a computer program capable of turning out anyone's horoscope instantly, given their date and hour of birth as input. (When Ruth Handler decided to produce an artificial breast for mastectomy patients, she sought out a top prosthetics expert, Peyton Massey, to design the product.)

• You make a connection that puts you in touch with a promising *product.*

Example: One of my public-relations clients was a friend of the inventive genius Bill Lear, designer of the Learjet. After Lear's death I made a point of asking one of Lear's top assistants if he knew of any invention worthy of development. Turned out he did—a device for increasing the fuel efficiency of automobile engines. And what could be more timely? By making a connection at the right moment, I procured an option to develop the device commercially.

• You make an ingenious new connection between a *known product* and a *known market.*

Example: A girlfriend of my daughter is addicted to attending garage sales and to shopping at flea markets. Since garage sales are transitory and flea markets more or less permanent, she got the idea of buying up merchandise at garage sales and reselling it, profitably marked up, at local flea markets. Her idea panned out so well that she now makes a full-time business out of it.

• You make a connection between a *new product* and a *known market.*

Example: We all know the major car-rental companies. They charge up to sixty dollars a day for their brand-new, shiny, clean cars; the average is about thirty dollars. Well, Dave Schwartz of Los Angeles hit on a very profitable idea when he said people would be glad to save money and ride around in a car that may not necessarily be new and shiny. He started Rent-A-Wreck, and charges $11.95 to $14.95 to rent mechanically sound, clean cars. Who cares if the car has a dent or two? Look at the money you can save. Rent-A-

Wreck now has 120 franchised locations and is going strong. Anyone looking for a way to get around safely and cheaply is a potential customer. With this thought in mind, Schwartz, an observant person, dared to start this new—and apparently thriving—business. Makes sense, doesn't it?

- You make a connection that greatly *expands the market* for a *given product.*

    Example: As adviser to the West German government, I was asked to help a German brassiere manufacturer introduce his product line to the American market. Brassieres were a stock item, and there was no outstanding feature to distinguish his line from competitive American makes. My solution was to invent and patent a method of breast measurement so that bras could be fitted individually to the buyer, including slight differences between the right and left breasts. This unique sales advantage, although it did not amount to a very important improvement in design, nevertheless brought a flood of business to the German manufacturer and made his brand name famous overnight.

- You make a new kind of connection between a *known service* and a *known need.*

    Example: This is a particularly interesting example because it involves creative thinking on the part of both buyer and seller. My wife happens to be a nervous driver who doesn't mind taking the wheel for a short trip to the supermarket but who has no taste for highway traffic or crowded commuter trains. So whenever she joined me in town for dinner and the theater, she hired a limousine to bring her into New York City. One day, while chatting with the local meter maid, she learned that the woman's husband was an out-of-work taxi driver. My wife immediately got the idea of hiring him to drive her in her own car into the city. He leaped at the chance, and soon realized that he could offer the same relatively inexpensive service to other limousine customers. He is now a highly successful commercial chauffeur and doesn't need a car or taxi of his own.

• You make a connection between a *known need* and your own *original solution* to that need.

Example: Representatives from the supermarket chain Food Fair once went to Drexel University to ask if its engineering department could help them in controlling supermarket inventory. The dean of Drexel did not think it was within their charter to help with this problem. Bernard Silver, who taught electrical engineering, overheard the conversation and went back to his office, where he asked Joe Woodland, a teacher of mechanical engineering, how he would solve the problem. After developing a scanning system, they tried to sell it to Food Fair. Food Fair's board decided not to go into it, as it looked like too big a project. They then applied for a patent and tried to sell it to IBM. IBM made a small offer and then doubled it, but it was still not sufficient to warrant the sale of the scanning device. Philco called to ask if it was for sale, and Woodland put a high price on it. Philco said they would be in touch with him within twenty-four hours, which they were, and accepted the terms. Now Woodland is working for IBM in improving the scanning techniques, and IBM is paying a royalty to Philco. This is an excellent example of how someone made his own luck by merely keeping his ears open and applying his talents.

I could go on and on with such examples, but the foregoing should suffice to show the infinite range of possibilities open to any eager beaver with an idea.

Perhaps you noticed, by the way, how I spoke of "making a connection with a market" or "with a need" or "with a problem." This was only for the sake of brevity. Actually, of course, the connection is always made with a *person* or with *people* who have a need for a product or who constitute a market or share a common problem. Notice also how in all these cases of *made luck* or business success, the originator has added some *new twist* or *creative touch* of his own to generate a whole new flow of business.

A school friend of my son, who in his teens was the class clown, has created a niche for himself in the most competitive business in the world—show business.

Soon after graduating, John Burstein got a job on the floating hospital ship that was then anchored in New York, giving free medical attention to the poor. Because he played guitar, he was hired to entertain the children. Rather than rely on timeworn nursery stories, he worked up lively song routines aimed at teaching the children the basic rules of health. To add to the fun and help show kids how their own bodies worked, he wore a leotard with bones, muscles, and internal organs painted on it, and introduced himself as "Slim Goodbody."

From the very start, John never lost sight of his professional show-biz ambitions. But he was looking for a gimmick, a unique act that would lift him above the competition—the huge horde of would-be actors in New York—and free him from the dreary round of casting "cattle calls." He had a hunch, which soon proved correct, that Slim Goodbody might be the answer.

From schools and small club dates, he soon graduated to singing his songs on *Sesame Street.* Meanwhile, he made a record album, which was bought by Macmillan Book Clubs. His highly original costume got him write-ups in several magazines. McGraw-Hill asked him to do a children's book. Since then he has written more books and is now on *Captain Kangaroo* twice a week.

Thus, John Burstein, the high-school clown, has succeeded in show business by creating something no one else had to offer. Even before reaching the ripe old age of thirty, he is unique, acclaimed—and making money.

Another individual who knew how to capitalize on a great idea by making the right connection is David Smith of Atlanta. He started off selling encyclopedias, first in this country, then in Japan. The encyclopedias, which were in English, sold well to the Japanese, not only because of their hunger to know more about America but also as a prestige item for their bookshelves. As a premium, he included a record, obtained from *Reader's Digest*, explaining in both languages how to use the book.

Gradually he realized his customers were more eager to obtain the record than the encyclopedias. *Reader's Digest* was already selling mail-order language courses based on such records. Smith decided to create his own course and spared no efforts to make it as attractive as possible.

He hired experts from Harvard University to develop the course, switched to cassettes instead of records, and included a book with clever artwork featuring Walt Disney characters to demonstrate the language easily to the learner. To sell the product, he would call up students and businessmen, and arrange to meet them in a coffee shop to stage his presentation.

But no course is of much use without a chance to practice the language. Smith made every customer a member of Actual Live Experience (ALE). He arranged hotel-get-togethers and other seminars, and provided, twenty-four hours a day, American instructors on the telephone whom the students could call and converse with in English. He also provided English-speaking group trips all over the world for his customers, with enough savings on the group fares to pay for the course itself.

Today, David Smith's unique language courses cost $1,500 apiece, and his volume of business has grown to over $50 million a year in Japan and Brazil, which has a sizable Japanese population. In time, he plans to develop other courses and to expand his market to other countries:

Speaking of foreign countries, a woman in our town who travels a lot has twice experienced the annoyance of having her luggage lost by the airline. The last time, she wasn't the only one on her flight to whom this happened— and suddenly she realized that nowadays lost luggage has become a common problem for air travelers.

In her own case the problem wasn't crucial, since she was returning home to a well-stocked dresser and closet. But what about the poor guy in a strange city who suddenly finds himself without a stitch except for the clothes he's wearing? Worse yet, he may be scheduled to stop over in that city for several days, with a tight schedule of activities in which he's expected to make a good appearance at all times.

By now that electric light bulb in her head had begun to glow. What about the big corporations in her vicinity, such as the Bell Laboratories or the Long Lines School, which the telephone company operates at Bedminster, New Jersey? With people flying in and out all the time, lost luggage must be a real problem.

Next day she was on the phone to these and other corporations, offering to supply the emergency clothing needs of employees who had lost their luggage in flight. Given a complete list of their measurements, she would shop for whatever items of clothing they wanted replaced—all selected and coordinated in good taste—deliver them in person, and even undertake to have the necessary alterations made promptly.

Since she first made the connection, her bright idea has

grown into a business. But it's no longer limited to people who have lost their luggage. She will undertake to assemble a complete, tastefully chosen wardrobe—or as many or as few garments as the customer desires—for people who dislike shopping for themselves.

I remember Prime Minister Ben-Gurion of Israel once joking with me about the problem of raising money for an urgently needed hospital. Everyone, he said, wanted to donate a wing or an operating theater, but nobody wanted to donate a lobby.

The Cathedral of St. John the Divine in New York City solved a similar problem in a unique, creative way. Instead of simply asking for financial contributions, the church inserted an ad in the Sunday New York *Times* inviting donors to contribute a particular piece of carved stone, such as an ashlar, quoin, or cornice, at prices ranging from one hundred to five thousand dollars.

By thus offering to immortalize their giving with an imperishable piece of masonry, the Episcopal Church has succeeded in making a connection with a whole new group of donors who might otherwise have remained unmoved by the church's solicitations.

Arco Publishing, which specializes in technical texts and now groses annually over $10 million, got started in a unique way. Milton Gladstone, its founder, first made a connection by hawking mimeographed copies of last year's tests to candidates waiting in line to take the civil-service exam for the job of U.S. Customs clerk. (Incidentally, the company got its name in an equally original way: The building it occupied still had a sign in front bearing the name of the previous occupant—ARCO.)

In Paris, in the early 1960s, a girl named Régine saw the growing popularity of rock music and sensed the urgent desire of the swinging younger generation for a nightclub of their own, where they could dance to music of their own taste. She had no money to hire a band or rent a decent-sized hall. But she knew a simple way to get the biggest names in music to entertain her guests—and, after all, rock-style dancing didn't require a lot of floor space. So she made the connection just by playing records—in a setup so tiny it became known as the Pipi Room. The result was the first disco. Her discos are now all over the world.

Over the years, the kind of nightclub she had invented grew into big business. In New York, besides an amplified, eardrum-shattering beat, a new element was added to the mix—the frenzied desire of people, even at the top-most social and economic level, to be part of the "in" crowd.

No one saw this more clearly than a formerly unsuccessful rock promoter. Born on New York City's Lower East Side, the son of a man whose headless body was found floating in Jamaica Bay, he was flat broke and out of a job. But he made the connection by talking a nightclub owner into financing a new disco.

Almost overnight, the disco became a smash success, with well-heeled customers clamoring on the sidewalk to get in. Today the rock promoter is a millionaire—all because he had an *idea* and turned it into a reality by making a connection.

Let me summarize. We've talked about needs; we've talked about ways to fulfill them. But the bottom-line success of any luck-making idea always depends on *people.*

Your idea isn't worth a red cent unless and until you get your product or service channeled to the persons who are going to use it—and the first step in doing that is to *make a connection.*

That's all this thing called business—any business—is about, from the world's oldest profession to the frontier peddler, hawking his goods from village to village and farm to farm. It holds true for him, and for you, just as surely as it holds true for the world's biggest corporation with glittering executive suites in a Manhattan skyscraper.

Flea markets were old hat in Europe and North Africa. But who ever heard of a flea market here in the United States, where we pride ourselves on our standard of living and our gleaming, machine-made products?

Someone knew better. He set up a flea market, rented stall space to various merchants, and cleared a tidy profit. He not only had the *idea*—secondhand junk pawed over by typical middle-class Americans—he made the connection between dealer and buyer.

Americans' discarded used clothing used to be shipped to poverty areas, such as Africa. Now it's being cleaned, mended, pressed—and profitably sold to middle-class Englishmen, who are eager for American styles but can't afford much in the way of new clothes. How did this come about? Someone got a fix on product and user, and made the connection.

Obsolete military gear is useless junk as long as it's gathering dust in government warehouses. But move it into local Army and Navy surplus stores, and the result is a multimillion-dollar industry—again because someone made the connection.

The same principle holds true in every aspect of business.

There's one last thought I'd like to leave in your mind: It's simple and easy to make connections if you keep your eyes and ears open and stay alert.

Business, you see, is like electricity. Before current can flow, there must be a complete path of wiring—a circuit—from power source to load. If a switch is open or a wire is loose, you'll get no current. To start it flowing, you must make the connection.

And when you do, you'll also be turning on your luck.

HOMEWORK

In this chapter I listed a number of different types of connections, along with examples of each. Try to match these with real-life examples of your own. For instance, one example involved an unemployed taxi driver who built a business chauffeuring people who don't want to drive their own cars and who would otherwise rent expensive limousines. I called this making a new kind of connection between a known service and a known need.

Can you come up with a similar idea that might work in your own community? Ditto for all the other categories I listed. One of the matching ideas you come up with may well provide *you* with the very opportunity you've been waiting for to *make a profitable connection.*

9

Figure Out Your Circuit

*I*n the last chapter we talked about making a connection—that is, getting in touch with another person as a first step in bringing your idea to life.

I used the analogy of an electrical circuit. Contacting that other person is like closing a switch or touching two wires together. It causes a current of energy to start flowing that can help you turn your luck-making idea into reality.

This, of course, comprises just a one-to-one circuit—you and the other person. In actual practice few circuits are that simple.

Say you plug an electric clock into an outlet. Chances are there are also various lights on that same circuit—not to mention an air conditioner, a TV set, perhaps other appliances as well. Not until you blow a fuse or pop a circuit breaker do you realize just how many gadgets are connected to that one electrical circuit.

And that circuit is just part of your home's wiring, which, in turn, is part of a larger hookup covering your whole block or neighborhood—as you discover when a storm at night knocks down a power line and you look out the window and see that lights have gone out, not just in your own house but in the houses all around you.

That neighborhood wiring is part of a still larger hook-up branching out from a relay station, where transformers step down the voltage of the electricity being brought in over long-distance transmission lines, which in turn are connected to the power plant where the electricity is first generated.

Only when a huge metropolis such as New York City suddenly blacks out, as happened in 1977, can most of us really understand just how large a power network our own individual living spaces are a part of. A network covers not just one state, but a whole region or even more than one country, as was dramatized when power had to be brought in from Canada to help get New York running again.

It's exactly the same way with human contacts. To generate your own luck, you may start by making a connection with one person. But a whole *chain of contacts* may have to be hooked up before your luck actually happens.

At first you'll probably have to make each such connection by yourself. But in time—as you go on making more and more connections in order to turn on more and more luck—you'll gradually build up a *permanent network* of contacts. Often you'll find that current will start flowing spontaneously through these contacts—and this flow of current can bring you dividends and benefits you never expected.

Let me give you an example.

One day, I went to see my printer about a particular job of work. While I was there he put me in touch with someone I'll call Mr. A. who handles the inserts for the monthly billings of a famous mail-order house. These inserts are combination ads and order forms for various products. No doubt you've seen them. You probably get several such inserts enclosed with every monthly credit-card bill that comes to you through the mail.

One of my own current projects, as I've already mentioned, is a medical newsletter that is distributed through various direct-mail channels. I asked Mr. A. if he would be interested in adding my newsletter to his list of products. At first his reaction was negative. But when we talked face to face and I showed him what I had to offer, his interest was aroused. He promised to recommend my medical newsletter to the mail-order house that employed him.

Several weeks later, I got a phone call from a Miss B. at the mail-order house in question. She said her company was interested in my newsletter and invited me to come to Chicago for a meeting on the subject.

But—and here's the kicker—she had *not* become aware of my newsletter through A.'s recommendation.

This is where the circuit starts to spread out.

Several months earlier, I had offered my newsletter to a syndicator who supplies mail-order products to credit-card companies (in this case an oil company). Keeping our names alphabetical, let's call the syndicator Mr. C.

Now, it so happened that Mr. C. had turned down my earlier proposal. Reason: His client was already offering a medical newsletter to its customers. But he and I knew each other well and had done business in the past, so he mentally filed my proposal.

Then something unexpected happened. The publisher of the oil company's newsletter went broke. His newsletter ceased publication.

Meanwhile, Miss B. had asked Mr. C. to supply this newsletter to her mail-order house. "Sorry, that's been discontinued," he told her. "But a man named Gittelson is publishing a medical newsletter that I can recommend. Why not get in touch with him?"

So she did. That's why she was calling me now. In fact

she wasn't even aware that Mr. A. had also recommended my product to her.

When I mentioned this, she said, "Wait a minute," and proceeded to shuffle through a pile of correspondence on her desk. "Oh, yes, here it is," she announced presently. "And you're right. I see that he did recommend your newsletter, which naturally makes us all the more eager to consider it. Shall we make a date for that meeting here in Chicago?"

Needless to say, I accepted promptly. But the story doesn't end there.

Having learned from my friend Mr. C. about the failure of the rival medical newsletter, I contacted the oil company's mail-order manager, Mr. D. He was now faced with a major problem: Either refund the amount of the customers' unexpired subscriptions or else take on the job of putting out the newsletter, which his organization had no facilities for doing.

Would I be interested in taking over the publication? he inquired.

No, but I came back with a counterproposal. Why not offer *my* newsletter to his customers, with the option of canceling their subscriptions if they didn't find mine acceptable?

Hmm, this appealed to Mr. D. But it turned out his problem was not that simple. The publisher who had gone broke, he told me, published a *gourmet* newsletter as well, which the oil company was also distributing.

In other words, the oil company had *two* newsletters to replace.

Would I be interested, he asked, in taking over the gourmet newsletter, too?

Well, now, it just so happened that I had been deeply involved in various aspects of cookery and food preparation during my PR days. At that time I'd had extensive contact both with editorial personnel in this field and with food-product companies. Thus I felt I could do a successful job of producing a gourmet newsletter.

"Splendid," said Mr. D., and immediately made a date to meet me in Chicago to discuss details of the deal.

So, in a short space of time, I had acquired not one but *two* new mail-order outlets for my medical newsletter—*plus* a separate project of publishing a gourmet newsletter with a prefab list of customers.

All this by a simple process of making connections, which in time linked up into a complete circuit or network of contacts.

Let me play this back for you: G. (meaning myself, Gittelson) to C., then, later, G. to printer to A. to B., but, meanwhile, also B. to C. to G., and additionally C. to G. to D.

Result: two major strokes of luck from a veritable spiderweb of interlocking connections.

Incidentally, several years before all this happened, an editor named Maureen had been let go by the women's magazine she worked for, and I had been instrumental in helping her find a new job. Part of her work had involved the testing of recipes and the editing of culinary articles for the food pages of that women's mag.

So when I needed help in putting out a gourmet newsletter, I immediately knew where to turn. I called up Maureen and she agreed to handle the editorial chores on a moonlighting basis.

Thus the circuit or network continued to grow, bringing *her* luck as well.

Now, in practical terms, what does all this mean to *you?*

It means that once you make that first connection and start the juice flowing, you mustn't stop there. You must *follow through* and hook up the whole circuit that will be needed to bring your idea to fruition.

But don't get the idea that this is something you can bring about overnight, just by making two or three phone calls—at least, not if this is your first venture into luck making.

It may well be a process that will take days and weeks, perhaps even months, of patient information gathering, checking out facts, talking and persuading, and legwork—not to mention a certain amount of penny-pinching or money borrowing in order to develop and advertise your product or service. (But let me hasten to add that, on your first venture, I strongly recommend that you hold down any cash investment to as little as possible.)

On the other hand, now that I've tut-tutted and shaken my head and warned you about all the difficulties you may face in setting up your success circuit, don't be downhearted.

The truth is, sometimes success *can* come very quickly. If your idea is good, if your timing is right, and if all the elements are in place, it may take only a single connection to complete the circuit and start your current of luck flowing strongly.

A good example is the success story of a man named Elton Canzi. Elton was a woodworking hobbyist. He had a workshop so well equipped with power tools that his friends were constantly asking permission to use them.

One day a joking remark by his wife made an electric light bulb flash in his head: If other people were so eager to use his tools, why not charge them for the privilege?

Elton decided to give the idea a try. He put an ad in the local newspaper, offering to let hobbyists use his woodworking power tools for an hourly rate. He also sent out cards to manual training teachers to let their pupils know about his shop facilities.

Before long he was swamped with customers and his

machines were running full blast every evening and through the weekend. His next step was to offer supplies for sale, such as wood, nails, and screws. Then he set up a darkroom in his basement for photographic hobbyists; eventually he added auto-repair facilities at the rear of his property for amateur mechanics who wanted to fix their own cars.

Elton Canzi now has a thriving home business that he was able to start with very little initial effort. Why? Because all the elements of a complete business circuit were there in the first place. All it took was one simple connection—namely, getting in touch with prospective customers by means of a newspaper ad and postcards to manual-training teachers—in order to start his luck current flowing.

From there he expanded the business merely by hooking up other types of hobbyists into his already existing circuit.

Lyle Kenyon Engle has become a fabulous figure in the book-publishing industry. Lyle has put together a mammoth book-creating operation based on a simple two-part circuit, with himself as the connecting link.

He started out as a magazine fiction editor. The work, I gather, was neither very well paid nor very satisfying. Lyle, you see, had a genuine love of fiction. During childhood he had spent many years as an invalid, owing to a football injury. To pass the time he read avidly, devouring every exciting adventure and mystery yarn he could get his hands on.

He knew a good story when he saw one, and his head was teeming with plot ideas.

Normally there are three figures involved in publishing books of fiction—the writer, his literary agent, and the editor. Many publishing houses can't afford to have readers plow through the mountains of hopeless stuff that comes flooding in, unsolicited, just in the hope of finding one or two usable manuscripts.

Consequently editors tend to rely on literary agents to put them in touch with promising new writers. And the writers, in turn, rely on their agents to get editorial attention for their manuscripts. This gives literary agents a good deal of middle-man power. Yet most of them exercise that power rather timidly and passively. They try to find out what various editors want, and what various people can write; and then match them up as best they can.

Lyle Engle wasn't satisfied with such a modest role. His magazine experience had brought him in contact with both editors and writers. And his own head, as I've already remarked, was teeming with plot ideas. So Lyle decided to *create books* himself.

Being an enthusiastic salesman, he would first sell an idea for a novel to an editor. Then he would find a suitable writer to flesh out this idea into a book-length manuscript. He would also guarantee the writer payment in advance, which involved little or no risk on his part, since money would be forthcoming from the publishing company, anyhow, on acceptance of the first few chapters and an outline. What's more, as a book producer rather than a mere agent he could demand and get a fifty-fifty split with the writer on the book's earnings, instead of the usual 10 percent agenting fee.

Being smart and industrious, Lyle soon got a reputation for delivering the goods. Writers liked to work for him because an assignment from Lyle meant instant money. In the 1970s he created a historical fiction series that, because of timing and execution, became a tremendous best seller. This bull's-eye hit brought him eager requests from other publishers for similar book series. Equally ambitious projects followed. He not only oversaw these projects from ideas to finished books, he even matched the publishers' promotional budgets with money of his own to promote the books he developed.

Today Lyle Engle is a millionaire many times over, and has probably created more books than any other man alive—even though he himself has never written a single one. His success, let me emphasize, is based on *completing a circuit,* which thereby caused his luck to flow—copiously.

Let's look at a few more examples.

Dan Renn was a young law-school dropout in North Carolina. He'd worked as a door-to-door salesman, hospital orderly, and teacher, and at various other jobs. Then in his mid-twenties, he seemed to be going nowhere fast.

One day his father-in-law showed him a fire-alarm device that he'd bought by mail. It was about as simple as anyone could possibly imagine—just a can of compressed gas, a horn, and a metal plug. When the temperature got hot enough, the plug would melt and the gas would expand and blow the horn.

Dan was fascinated by the foolproof simplicity of the design. He sensed almost immediately that here was a sure-selling item. A lot of other people may have felt the same way—but they did nothing about it. Dan Renn, however, *made a connection.* He wrote to the manufacturer—Falcon Safety Products, Inc., in New Jersey—and went to see them in person.

At that time the little company was getting off to a slow start. It was only too happy to acquire an enthusiastic new rep in North Carolina. Dan came home with the right to sell the device on commission in the Winston-Salem area.

Then he set about *completing the circuit* from maker to user—and sold alarms to the first twenty householders he called on. Within a year he was rich.

He began enlarging the circuit, at first by recruiting other salesmen to work for him, then by incorporating his sales organization as Renn Enterprises, Ltd., and expanding to other cities and states. Within another year sales had quintupled. His company's volume grew so fast that it finally took over as national distributor and sales agent for Falcon Safety Products and began spreading out across the country. By the time he was thirty Dan Renn was a millionaire.

Elsie Frankfurt and her sister Edna were two Texas girls, daughters of a Dallas real-estate man. Elsie was just out of college, where she'd studied dress designing and accounting; Edna was married and visibly pregnant.

At that time there were no maternity clothes to speak of, and one day, when Edna dropped over for a visit, she was wearing an old wraparound dress of their mother's for lack of anything better.

Then and there, Elsie decided to make her sister a new outfit. She solved the design problem by cutting a U-shaped opening in the skirt to fit around the unfittable tummy bulge. A loose-fitting smock went over it; the outfit was as comfortable as it was attractive. Pregnant friends wanted one like it. Women would stop Edna on the street to ask where she'd got it.

An electric light bulb lit up in Elsie's head as she realized that here was an idea they might patent and use to start a business. The two girls scraped up five hundred dollars, rented shop space in a medical-arts building where many obstetricians practiced, bought enough fabric for a dozen dresses, and hired a seamstress to make them at home. Thus they set up a *complete circuit* for their product, from production to consumer. The sign on the door said PAGE BOY.

Business thrived from the start. A customer wore one of their dresses to Atlanta, where she was spotted by a specialty-shop buyer who wound up ordering eighteen dresses. A friend brought back an order for twenty-four outfits from Best & Company in New York, then got other orders for more than a hundred dresses from several department-store buying offices.

Suddenly Page Boy was no longer a shop turning out its own product. It had become a big business, wholesaling as well as retailing. Production was shifted to a factory loft with ten sewing machines. In its very first year the company grossed $100,000.

Always, the sisters kept *expanding their circuit.* They established credit with big fabric companies in order to obtain adequate supplies at businesslike prices. They opened a New York showroom, other shops in Los Angeles, San Francisco, and various other cities, and eventually erected their own building in Dallas to house factory, offices, and retail shop.

Both Elsie and Edna, as well as their younger sister, Louise, who joined the firm after college, are now millionaires.

Let me interject another thought here. Don't get the idea that there's anything terribly mysterious or difficult about hooking up a circuit to make your own luck. If you know what you're trying to achieve, as often as not the right steps to achieve it will occur to you naturally. All it takes to figure out your next move is common sense. One step follows another.

In fact, sometimes just that first step of making a connection may lead directly to your circuit hookup.

For example, one night I was watching the Merv Griffin show. The guest was a scientist. He was deeply into vitamin therapy and had worked out a vitamin formula that he was convinced could stave off disease—and even old age. He believed this formula could also prolong human life. As he talked he held the studio audience spellbound.

That old electric light bulb began flashing brilliantly in my head. Vitamins and vitamin therapy were already a popular, marketable commodity. But here was the ultimate in sales appeal. What human yearning could ever be more powerful or universal than the desire for eternal youth?

Next day I called the Merv Griffin people and found out how to get in touch with the scientist. When I phoned him, he proved affable and stimulating to talk to. "Sure, stop in next time you're in town," he said.

I said, "That'll be as soon as I can catch a plane."

To make a long story short, we met and had a long, intensely interesting conversation.

"I think your vitamin formula has commercial possibilities," I told him. "I'd like to discuss marketing it."

The first formula is now undergoing clinical tests and may soon be available nationwide.

The important thing I want to emphasize here is the simplicity of what happened.

With two absolutely cold phone calls I made a *direct connection* with a person who had something unusual to offer the public. This connection led directly to a *circuit hookup*.

Obviously there were numerous details involved, and there will be many more before the vitamin preparation reaches the market. The scientist has no financial interest in the formula. He just wanted to see it made available.

My reason for telling you all this is not to dwell on the commercial possibilities that will doubtless ensue. My point is that by watching a television show that was being seen by millions of people all over America, I immediately sensed an angle that could generate a lot of *luck*. Perhaps other viewers sensed that angle, too—I'll never know for sure. But out of all those viewers, I was the *only one* who followed up and did anything about it withour hours.

You, too, may be able to hook up a luck-making circuit just as swiftly and easily—*if* you'll get up off the seat of your pants, whenever you spot a promising idea, and start *doing* something about it by making that first connection.

What do you need to do to hook up a complete luck making circuit? Generally speaking, there are three early tasks:

1. *Find out all you need to know about the product or service you hope to provide.* If you yourself know zilch about the subject to start with, talk first to any knowledgeable friends. Have them suggest other people who can tell you still more. Go to your local library. It's a treasure trove of information about every subject. In this way find out who are the very top experts on the subject—and don't hesitate to contact them cold, if necessary, if you can't find any way to arrange an introduction. In short, go straight to the horse's mouth. And while you're at it, don't neglect to research the subject from the *consumer's* end as well. Talk to a few of your hoped-for, future customers. Find out just how eager they are for this product or service you plan to provide. If it were available today, how readily would they shell out money to pay for it?

2. *Contact people who can help you develop your product or service.* This may include manufacturers or wholesalers or retail stores from which you can obtain the supplies you need to turn out your products. Find out how you can get the best material most cheaply and quickly, preferably at wholesale prices. Once they see you as an important future customer, these suppliers may go out of their way to lend you a hand in getting started. If your idea involves a service rather than a product, you may need partners or helpers in

order to offer that service to the public. Again, by contacting such people, you may get important help on your project at the very outset.

3. *Contact the people who will use your product or service.* You may already have gotten in touch with some of them at the information-gathering stage of your project. But once you go into business, you will need to contact them on a much wider scale in order to inform them that whatever you have to offer is now available at a reasonable price. This may involve some form of *advertising*—in your local newspaper, by direct mail, by printed handbills, or by posting a sign on the bulletin board of your local supermarket; or it may involve *telephone prospecting*—calling names at random from the phone book or whatever kind of selection may suit your marketing needs; or it may require *face-to-face contact,* such as door-to-door selling, the parking-lot approach, and so forth.

Once you've adequately covered these three areas, you should be well on your way toward establishing your basic circuit hookup. In the next couple of chapters I'll give you some down-to-earth, red-meat ideas on *how* to cover them effectively.

10

Rev Up Your Generator

What makes a great prizefighter?

Obviously, a knockout punch. Lots of heart. Boxing finesse. Ring savvy. And, above all, *speed*, the ability to *react fast*—to get out of the way before his opponent's punches connect and to score with his own fists before his opponent can duck.

What are the characteristics of a skilled luck maker?

Here again, one of the most important is *speed*, the ability to *react fast*, to get moving on your idea . . .

- while it's still sizzling hot in your mind
- before your enthusiasm cools
- before you forget all about it
- before the dim-sighted, envious, unimaginative plodders all around you have time to infect you with their own inertia
- before they convince you that it's really not much of an idea after all and will probably never pay off.

Remember, earlier on, when I told you how Milton Gladstone, the founder of Arco Publishing Company, got started on his multimillion-dollar career as a textbook publisher? In case you've forgotten, let me run it past you again because it's a perfect example of fast timing—spotting a promising idea and following up on it immediately while the door of opportunity is wide open.

Milton had gone to get his motor-vehicle license renewed at the state office building and found himself in a long line of people stretching all around the lobby. The wrong line, as it turned out. These people were waiting to apply for a limited number of civil-service jobs as clerks.

He noticed some of the applicants poring over copies of last year's exam for this position. He learned that these copies had been on sale in the lobby for fifteen cents apiece, but now were all gone.

An electric light bulb flashed—and he reacted immediately.

"Hey," said Gladstone to the youth in front of him, "I'll give you a dollar for your copy."

The youth shook his head. "Nothing doing. I want to bone up on these questions. It'll give me a better chance of passing the exam."

Gladstone upped his offer to two dollars. Still no sale.

But somebody else in line had overheard Gladstone and eagerly held out his own copy. "Here," he said, "you can have mine for two bucks."

Gladstone bought it on the spot, went home, and filled out the answers to all the questions. They weren't too difficult. The answers he couldn't supply himself, he looked up or found out. Then he mimeographed several hundred copies of the completed exam.

Next morning he was back in the building lobby as the

line began to form. Gladstone started to hawk his wares: "Get your copies of last year's exam—with all the answers. Just two bits for a head start on your competition."

The demand was so great that he sold out in no time and had to mimeograph some more copies.

This happened during the Great Depression, when jobs were as scarce as hen's teeth. Applications for the civil-service openings were taken over a ten-day period, during which time long lines continued to form from early morning and throughout the day. And Milton Gladstone continued to hawk his mimeographed questions and answers to last year's exams. They sold like hotcakes.

Incredibly, by the time it was all over, he had cleared *three thousand dollars.*

And there, as I said before, you have a classic example of a speedy reaction to a promising opportunity. Gladstone didn't have to rev up his generator. He went from idea to execution in nothing flat.

He made his first *contact* when he bid two dollars for one of the sold-out copies of last year's exam. He *completed the circuit* when he started selling his mimeographed questions and answers.

Consciously, I'm sure, Gladstone never stopped to analyze what he was doing in terms of contact or circuit. He simply heard opportunity knocking and let it in pronto before it passed him by.

While we're at it, please notice how neatly this exemplifies all the elements of the luck-making process:

1. *Gladstone recognized an urgent need or desire.* The civil-service–job applicants had shown a willingness to pay hard cash for a copy of last year's examination. But now the copies were all gone. Yet applicants would continue lining up for days to come, and they would no doubt be just as

eager to buy copies as those who had preceded them.

2. *Gladstone saw a better way to fulfill that need.* Presumably he could have gone through official channels and obtained more copies of the exam from the U.S. Printing Office, but this would have been time consuming and relatively costly. How much cheaper and quicker it was just to mimeograph the questions. And not only the questions; why not add a new element—the answers?

3. *Gladstone did something about his idea.* He shelled out two dollars for a fifteen-cent copy of the printed exam, purely in the interest of speed. He was back first thing in the morning with hundreds of mimeographed copies of the questions and answers. And he continued to supply the buyers with what they wanted for the remainder of the application period.

The story doesn't end there, by the way. Having seized and capitalized on one opportunity, Gladstone immediately recognized that similar luck-making opportunities existed, month after month and year after year, whenever the civil service advertised new job openings.

But from here on, he didn't rely on last-minute mimeographing. He started obtaining, well ahead of time, copies of last year's examination, not just for one job classification in a single government department but for all kinds of jobs in all the government departments. Then he had them printed, along with the answers, in textbook format.

Publishers get excited when a popular new novel sells hundreds of thousands of copies. It was years before they gradually realized that Milton Gladstone's Arco Publishing Company was routinely selling millions of copies of plain old textbooks, which had cost him almost nothing to compile in the first place.

By the time other publishers decided to get in on the bonanza, Gladstone was ready to get out. He sold Arco for a price well up in the millions.

Getting back to our original point—namely, speedy reaction to a promising idea: *Promptly* is always the best way to carry out the luck-making process, for several reasons.

Enthusiasm is an essential ingredient in making your own luck. And invariably you'll find that your own enthusiasm is at a peak when that electric light bulb flashes on in all its dazzling brilliance.

The longer you sit around and twiddle your thumbs before doing anything about it, the more that enthusiasm is bound to ebb. Doubts will start creeping in, one by one—slowly at first, then in a swelling flood, until you become more and more convinced that your big idea doesn't stand a chance.

If you've told others about your idea, they'll probably think of a dozen reasons why it would never work—in fact, why it was never any good in the first place.

None of which is true. Unless and until you actually try out an idea, nobody can say for sure just how good it is—because *nobody knows*. But that won't stop people from telling you your idea's no good. (Can you imagine how many people would have told the Wright brothers they were wasting their time—that that silly-looking contraption would never get off the ground?)

Just remember that a large percentage of such negative reaction, whether the people realize it or not, stems from envy and resentment. Envy of you for having the brains, a creative drive, and ambition to think up such a possible luck-making idea. Resentment of you because, never having been touched by the golden wand of luck themselves, they can't stand the thought of your doing better than they and thus making them look like fools by comparison. So they'll do their damnedest to turn you off.

Another reason it's important to get moving fast on an idea is *momentum.* When you first become excited and enthusiastic about a new concept, your body is all revved up to go into action. That's what enthusiasm is—it's energy seeking an outlet.

When you're angry, you're revved up to fight. When you're fearful, you're revved up to flee from danger. When you're enthusiastic, you're revved up to do something about whatever has inspired your enthusiasm.

Therefore, by moving promptly on an idea, you're taking advantage of an impulse that's already churning inside you, trying to propel you toward your goal. All you have to do is open the throttle and let 'er rip. It's like leaping aboard a moving bus. You get carried along by the emotional momentum your idea has already generated.

On the other hand, if you just sit there on your fanny and daydream, all that powerful motivating force will go to waste. Oh, sure, you may say, "Tomorrow I'll get on it," or "Next week I'll call so-and-so and start things moving." Fine. Let's hope you do.

The only catch is, if you wait till tomorrow or next week, you won't be starting out with the same head of steam. Instead of leaping aboard a moving bus, you'll first have to get the bus moving again—from a dead stop. And as any engineer will tell you, it takes much more energy to nudge a stationary vehicle into motion than it does to keep a moving vehicle rolling along.

Realistically, of course, there may be times when you can't leap into action on an idea. You may really be too busy. The idea may have hit you when you were up to your eyeballs in some other project. You may need more time to think out all the angles. The one person you need to get in touch with may be out of town.

Well and good—so long as you're not just rationalizing to excuse your own laziness or to justify an unnecessary delay.

In the meantime, there's at least one thing you *can* do: Write down your idea.

And don't be satisfied with just a simple, bald statement of the idea. Use your pen or pencil to "think on paper." Figure out a plan of action. Decide what your initial step should be. Pinpoint your first connection. Lay out your circuits. If you're going to have to persuade or convince someone to back your project, then organize your presentation.

In fact, it's often a productive move to work out an imaginary presentation even if you don't have to persuade or convince anyone. In this way you'll force yourself to think through every aspect of the subject. What exactly is the public need or desire you're going to satisfy? How will your idea uniquely meet this need or desire? Why would anyone be willing to pay money for the product or service you propose to offer?

Then reread what you've just written. Tear it apart and criticize it from every possible angle. You're now ready to rewrite your presentation for maximum effectiveness. And by doing so, I can practically guarantee that you'll sharpen and improve your idea a hundred percent—or, if not the idea itself, then at least your ability to carry it out successfully.

Now, why all this emphasis on speed and momentum?

It's for a very good reason: These are the most effective strategies against the single greatest obstacle that prevent most people from making their own luck.

That obstacle is *inertia*—the sit-back-and-do-nothing

syndrome. Believe me, I speak from years of experience and observation when I say that this factor more than any other is what keeps most people plodding along in the same old rut and stops them from ever moving out ahead of the common herd.

Mind you, this syndrome doesn't necessarily imply laziness, though that may well play a part in the overall result—or, rather, in the overall lack of result. Much more often, though, I believe inertia is due to such causes as timidity, shyness, self-doubt, reluctance to be different, unwillingness to "rock the boat"—even outright fear.

We pride ourselves on living in a democratic society where every individual is encouraged to do his own thing. A brave ideal. But, in fact, from the day we are born, every one of us is subjected to intense pressures aimed at making us conform to the norm.

As adults we tend to speak irritably or disparagingly of the "peer pressures" to which teenagers are subjected—their need to be like everyone else in their crowd, which may induce them to drink and drive recklessly or experiment with drugs or indulge unwisely in sex, thereby adding to the number of pregnant teenagers and unwed mothers.

Why are they such idiots? we wonder. Why haven't they the self-respect and backbone to behave sensibly and refuse to go along with the crowd?

The truth is, we adults are every bit as guilty of mass conformity and yielding to peer pressures as any teenager.

Can you remember when every grown-up American male cut his hair short and shaved his sideburns high and went off to work at his office job in the same kind of neat, business-suited uniform? Even at home his leisure clothing consisted mostly of shirt sleeves, no tie, and old trousers.

It took the hippies of the 1960s to liberate American men from all that. Without their bold example, what adult male in his right mind would ever have dared to grow a beard, or go to work with his hair curling down over his shirt collar, or be seen cutting the grass in the gaudy sport shirt and slacks or shorts now favored by the typical male suburbanite?

Women are almost as bad in their passive willingness to conform and be dictated to by the czars and czarinas of fashion.

The point I'm getting at here is that the process of making your own luck does often require you to break step with the herd and step out into exposed view all by yourself, where people can point at you and jeer and make fun of your ideas.

Don't kid yourself for a minute that people with new ideas to propose have an easy time of it. There seems to be something about the human animal *en masse* that often makes him almost savagely hostile to anyone who challenges the accepted way of doing things.

Dr. Ignaz Semmelweis, who studied puerperal fever, was denounced by other medics as an outrageous quack for daring to suggest that doctors themselves often fatally infected new mothers when, on coming directly from infectious wards or working on cadavers, they delivered babies without first washing their hands.

In the early years of this century, suffragettes in this country and in England were often imprisoned and humiliatingly force-fed for daring to demonstrate on behalf of women's right to vote.

A few years back, when gold had risen to the astounding price of more than one hundred dollars an ounce, I remember seeing an economic forecaster on a TV show draw amused chuckles from his fellow "experts" when he predicted that continued inflation would send gold prices soaring past five hundred dollars an ounce. You could almost hear them muttering to each other, "What a nut," or "The guy's so hipped on that one subject he's obviously gone off his rocker."

Subsequently gold went as high as seven hundred dollars an ounce.

Every rocket shot into space is equipped with numerous engineering features invented by America's greatest pioneering rocket expert, Dr. Robert Goddard. Yet his work was largely ignored by our own military. Meanwhile, the Germans were gratefully and successfully applying his discoveries in their deadly V-2 rocket program during World War II.

In 1945 our top civilian wartime scientist and presidential adviser, Dr. Vannevar Bush, was pooh-poohing the very idea of intercontinental ballistic missiles. He actually testified before a Senate committee that, "In my opinion such a thing is impossible for many years to come. . . . I think we can leave that out of our thinking. I wish the American public would leave that out of their thinking."

Eleven years later, when the U.S. satellite program had already begun and only months before the first Russian Sputnik was successfully launched into orbit, England's Astronomer Royal snorted, "Space travel is utter bilge."

These were experts speaking, mind you. Typical examples of what the *New Yorker* magazine likes to call the "Clouded Crystal Ball."

Along about the same time that satellites were first being rocketed into space, a world-famous psychiatrist, Dr. Wilhelm Reich, was dying heartbroken in a federal prison. He had been convicted of fraud for his orgone-box therapy. Today, his ideas are receiving fresh and serious consideration by respected scientists in his field.

Not so long ago, an inspector for a major manufacturer of military equipment publicly drew attention to certain slipshod manufacturing practices prevailing in the company he worked for. These practices wasted both company and public money. To a certain extent, they threatened the lives of American military personnel who used the equipment. Was he thanked or rewarded for trying to correct these shortcomings in the only way available to him? On the contrary, he was fired by his employer and ostracized by his neighbors and fellow workers.

Yes, no doubt it's true that I've picked out some particularly horrifying examples to dramatize my point, which is that any innovator can expect to encounter a certain amount of hostile resistance and even ridicule. Nevertheless, it's also true that it does take gumption and guts to step out on your own and blaze a brand-new trail across the public landscape—or even just to tell your boss that you've thought up a better way to do things around the office than they're now being done under his managerial eye.

To stick your neck out in this way, you must literally dare to be different. And that scares some people. As I said, this is one important reason that so few ever do stray off the reservation, so to speak—why many never venture to back a new idea or voice an independent thought or aim their lives in a new direction.

It's so much safer and easier, you see, to stay huddled down in your own snug little rut and go plodding along in a straight line until the boss hands you an engraved watch for umpty-ump years of loyal service and you totter off into retirement with the reassuring knowledge that you never took an unnecessary risk in your life.

What about *you?*

Have you the gumption to strike off in some new direction on your own?

Are you ready to start relating to people in brand-new ways?

Are you capable of injecting new romance into your marriage by behaving differently and more attentively and understandingly toward your spouse?

Are you brave enough to risk the jealous resentment of your fellow employees by devising and proposing new, more efficient working procedures to your boss?

Have you the nerve to approach some business big shot and suggest a way in which you think he can increase his sales or profits?

Can you ring people's doorbells and convince them they need your product or service?

Be honest with yourself in answering these questions. Only God and you need ever know what your answers are. I can't emphasize too strongly that if you have a problem in this area, now is the time to find out and face it.

By this time, if you've read through all the preceding chapters, you've probably come up with at least one or two promising ideas for improving your luck—right?

Well, then, if so, have you tried turning any of them into reality yet?

If not, why not? What's holding you back?

This, you see, is the true *bottom line* of making your own luck. No amount of tips or instruction that I can give you from my own experience about how to get the right kind of ideas and put them to effective use will do you the slightest bit of good—unless and until you get up off the seat of your pants and do something about them.

So long as you sit back and do nothing, nothing will happen. You'll go on, day after day, week after week, year after year, plodding along in the same old rut. You'll go on being one of the common herd, cursing the dark and complaining about your own lack of luck.

But it'll actually be your own fault for doing nothing.

By the same token, once you do start *acting* instead of

daydreaming, your battle is already half won. When that happens, you really won't even need this book in order to make your own luck.

Given an average amount of intelligence, you see— plus a willingness to keep trying and learn from your own mistakes—you can hardly help but improve your position in life.

Sure, you may flounder and fall on your face a few times, just as you did when learning to skate or ride a two-wheeled bike. But sooner or later you'll master the knack, and then it's only a matter of time before you'll be well on the road to success.

This book can, I hope, smooth the way and speed up your progress. But the fact remains that propelling yourself into action is the single most important step in the whole process. And you alone can accomplish that step.

This is why I called this chapter "Rev Up Your Generator."

Without that inner spark or drive to energize you into making your first move, what's the good of talking about making a connection or laying out your success circuit? As long as you fail to act on your idea, nothing will happen.

But once you do rev yourself into action, nothing can stop you. Now try the test below:

1. Pick out the most promising idea you've come up with so far.

2. Write it down as suggested earlier, so you'll know exactly what to do.

3. Set a deadline by which you resolve to put your idea into action.

4. If the deadline passes and you've done nothing, ask yourself what excuses you have to offer.

5. If your excuses appear valid, give yourself another chance. Set another deadline for action.

6. If that second deadline passes and you've still done nothing, don't bother making any more excuses. The time has now come to ask yourself in all candor: Do I really want to succeed? Only you can answer that question.

Let me tell you about three determined people.

A painter named Pieter Molereld caught polio and had to be put in an iron lung. But that didn't defeat him or stop him from practicing his art. He learned to foot-paint and acquired the same mastery with a brush that he had displayed before when he was still able to use his hands.

Guerrino Collina lost both his arms through illness. He learned to mouth-paint. Eventually his work was shown in many exhibitions and he became a professional art teacher.

Denise Legrix, a French woman, was born without either arms or legs. She taught herself not only painting but sewing, embroidery, and typing.

Kelly Barfoot was born without legs and is missing two fingers of his right hand, but he fishes, hunts, plays trumpet in an amateur band, drives his father's tractor, and is a medical student at the University of Missouri–Kansas School of Medicine. He gets around campus on a skateboard, which he propels with his hands. When he makes his rounds in the hospital, he wears artificial legs and uses crutches.

Do you want to succeed in life as badly as Pieter Molereld, Guerrino Collina, Denise Legrix, and Kelly Barfoot wanted to overcome their respective handicaps?

If you do, you'll learn to make your own luck and eventually you will succeed.

If you don't, you won't.

It's as simple as that.

Assuming you do indeed want to make your own luck and improve your situation in life—yet you have trouble overcoming passivity or timidity—here are four suggestions that may help you get moving.

FIRST SUGGESTION

Back in the mid-1970s, with the war in Vietnam ended and the United States grappling with the first pangs of recession and inflation, our national aerospace program was drastically cut back. Thousands of highly trained engineers were suddenly thrown out of work. Many were middle-aged or, at any rate, no longer young enough to be readily employable or adaptable to totally new types of employment. In any case there were few jobs to be had. As a result, they had to shift for themselves and make their own luck.

Not too pleasant a situation to be confronted with, one might think. Yet in reading newspaper reports of what happened to these engineers, I was left with the opposite impression.

For example, two ex–space engineers on the West Coast had gone into partnership and opened a highly successful antique shop in San Francisco. One aeronautical engineer on Long Island had become a landscape gardener. Another, in Washington State, was designing and hand-crafting jewelry.

What stood out clearly was the fact that most of the men interviewed sounded positively exhilarated by their new life-styles and experiences—almost as if they found themselves using muscles they never knew they had, and were enjoying it to the hilt. Not to mention the fact that many, now self-employed, were actually making more money in their new businesses than they had made while on company payrolls, and were now asking themselves why they'd never dared to take the plunge sooner.

Earlier, in the 1960s, the liberated life-styles of America's youth had tempted many uptight professional people to break away from their straitlaced roles and tackle jobs they would never have dared to think of taking on before, such as farming and weaving and running a country store. I recall reading about one computer programmer who formed a highly successful trash-collecting company. Among this group, too, reports seemed to show that the change in careers had generally resulted in happier, more satisfying lives.

So if you're leery or timid about striking out on your own and attempting to make your own luck, try revving yourself up by saying, "This move can help to make my life happier and more satisfying than ever before."

SECOND SUGGESTION

One of the greatest handicaps that nonachievers impose on themselves is their reluctance to believe that they can ever become successful.

I once had dinner with a man who had served in the U.S. Navy for twenty years before retiring on a pension after World War II with the grade of chief machinist's mate. He had worked all his life with his hands, yet for years he had cherished the dream of becoming a writer.

On leaving the Navy, he enrolled in college, taking all the English and other literature courses he could fit into his program, and at the same time he began trying to write science-fiction stories, his own favorite reading matter. Yet he told me that he never really believed he could make the grade until one summer he attended a science-fiction convention. Here he met other professional and would-be writers who talked to him freely and encouragingly, swapped experiences, and generally accepted him on his own terms. As a result, for the first time he actually began to believe that, with sufficient effort, he could someday become a successful writer.

This man went on to write a best-selling novel, which was not science fiction but a gripping and realistic adventure yarn about naval enlisted men serving in the China Station in the 1920s. The book, called *The Sand Pebbles,* made his fortune overnight and became a major motion picture starring Steve McQueen.

So if you're lethargic or fearful about reaching out for success, try revving up your generator by believing in yourself for a change.

THIRD SUGGESTION

Maybe you've come up with a red-hot idea that you'd like to present to the head of a certain company. Yet the prospect of talking to anyone that important makes you quiver with stage fright. Even the thought of conversing with such a big shot at the other end of a phone makes your throat go so dry you can't talk. And the very notion of being ushered into a company president's palatial office turns your knees to jelly.

Let me tell you something. In the first place, that company president is a guy who eats and excretes and gets nagged by his wife and puts on his pants one leg at a time just as you and I and others do.

Much more important, you're going to find him very receptive. In fact you're likely to find his ear the most eagerly listening ear in the whole company.

Does that surprise you? Well, always bear in mind that this man, more than anyone else, bears the prime responsibility of making money for his company's stockholders. His job depends on how well he does so.

As a result, he's always looking for ways to reduce expenses and increase his sales and profits. If you've got an idea that offers the slightest promise of helping him achieve those goals, believe me, he wants to hear it.

He doesn't give a damn if you're young or old, tall or short, fat or skinny, male or female, white, black, red, or yellow. The only thing that counts is what *you* have to offer.

Shortly after the Korean War I was called in as a consultant by a corporation that owned one of the biggest foundries in the United States. It had been built to turn out cannons for the Army. But now that the war was over, they had lost their government contracts. So what to do with the foundry? Did I have any ideas?

The company's own management had vague notions of producing some kind of tank. But from a practical standpoint the idea wasn't too promising. Certain smaller countries, such as Greece and Turkey, whose military programs were being financially aided by the United States, were eager to buy tanks. But our American models were too big and heavy for their bridges to support.

This gave me an idea. The French were building a smaller-size tank that the Israeli Army had used with smashing success in the Six-Day War. Greece, Turkey, and other of our allies would dearly have loved to buy such tanks. But the financial aid provided by the United States could be spent only on armaments purchased in this country.

But suppose the French could be persuaded to let their tank be built in this country. The millions of dollars spent on making these tanks would do them no good at all. On the other hand, 30 percent of the total project cost would be spent on replacement parts, and these parts could be sold by France.

In other words, although the French would lose out as

prime contractors, they would at least gain 30 percent of the business—which ultimately promised to amount to over a billion dollars.

The tank in question had actually been developed by a consortium of French manufacturers, including some of the most distinguished businessmen in Europe. I was then a young man, but it became my job to sell these big shots on the outrageous idea of giving away the manufacturing rights to their own prize tank model.

What did I do? First of all, I made contact with the head of the consortium through his American lawyer, who was politely cooperative but thought I had no chance whatever of achieving success.

I can still remember the amused way the head of the consortium looked at me when he received me in his magnificent office near Paris and listened to my proposal. Does this young idiot—he seemed to be thinking—actually believe he can persuade me to agree to such a ridiculous arrangement?

All the same, he listened while I explained and reasoned with him. And then he had me return to France and explain it all over again, not once but several times. And each time he would bring in another member of the consortium, equally amazed and amused, to hear my outrageous proposal.

Yet, believe it or not, the arrangement was finally agreed to and the contract signed, after two years of never giving up—because my proposal made sense.

Why? Because these fellows were keen, intelligent businessmen, and the bottom line was a matter of simple arithmetic—namely, 30 percent of $1 billion was $300 million more than nothing.

So if you're too shy or bashful or lacking in self-confidence to present your idea to the big shot you need to convince, rev up your generator by realizing that you'll find him not only receptive but eager to hear how your idea can help to improve his business.

FOURTH SUGGESTION

Maybe you've got a real whiz-bang of an idea that you actually believe could make millions. But the sheer scope of the idea intimidates you. How could you possibly tackle such a big deal? You'd need money, a large organization, contacts all over the country, and so forth. People would laugh at you for entertaining such delusions of grandeur.

Did you ever hear of a man named Charles Darrow? In 1933 he was an out-of-work heating engineer, not only jobless but broke. He supported his family with whatever odd jobs he could find, which included walking other people's dogs.

To cheer himself up he invented a game that involved speculating in real estate with a fortune in play money. He made the various pieces of the game. It was so much fun to play that people and neighbors paid him to make similar sets for them. Darrow was willing. He had nothing much else to do.

Orders started coming in so fast that he had to hire help. Eventually he showed the game to some local stores in his hometown, as well as to department stores in nearby Philadelphia. When one big store gave him an order for a wholesale lot, he finally copyrighted the game and farmed out production to a printer friend.

But business kept growing by leaps and bounds, and spreading far beyond Philadelphia. There was no possible way to keep up with demand, short of raising capital and starting up a large manufacturing operation. Instead, Darrow offered to license the game to Parker Brothers, the biggest producer in the game business.

At first they turned him down. The game seemed to

violate all their carefully established rules for successful table games. But as Christmas of 1934 approached and they saw how Darrow's business was exploding beyond all bounds, they hastily reconsidered and offered him a royalty contract that Darrow willingly signed.

Even Parker Brothers couldn't cope with the frantic demand at first. It became the biggest best seller the company ever produced. Darrow was able to retire for life less than three years after signing the royalty contract. And the profits kept pouring in, year after year. He died in 1970, a multimillionaire—and his heirs will doubtless go on receiving royalties for years to come.

The name of the game, in case you haven't already guessed it, is Monopoly.

Moral: If your idea seems too big and intimidating to tackle, *start small* and let it expand by its own momentum, sweeping you on to fame and fortune in the process.

11

Turn On the Juice

Okay, so you've come up with a brilliant inspiration that you think can make you lucky. What's more, you've gotten up off your duff and done something about it. You've made a connection and now you're ready to *turn on the juice*.

Presumably that means you're face to face, or soon will be, with someone who has the power to help turn your idea into reality—or snuff out your hopes with a shake of the head and a "Sorry, not interested."

How do you get that key individual to light up with enthusiasm, just as you yourself did when an electric light bulb suddenly flashed in your head?

I'd say the first step toward that goal is to make sure you're talking to the *right person*—someone with enough kilowatts or megawatts of power in his own organization to start your idea humming through a *complete business circuit*.

Obviously the company's security guard in the outer lobby or that attractive receptionist can't do you any good in this respect. The president's secretary might if she's his active assistant in everything but name, or some vigorous young exec who functions as the boss's right-hand man in implementing and carrying out new projects.

But, generally speaking, the right person to contact in any given setup is the head honcho himself. So let's make this . . .

RULE NUMBER 1

Insist on talking to the head man

As I've already explained, the head man is not only the person who has the final say about accepting or rejecting your idea, he's also likely to be the most receptive person you can deal with, the closest, most sympathetic ear.

This has nothing to do with his personal charm or tact or patience or intelligence. He may be the gruffest, surliest oaf you ever met—a mixture of Simon Legree and Scrooge, who wouldn't toss a stale crust to a starving beggar. What matters is that he's also the person with the greatest incentive to scout out promising new ideas that can boost his company's business or expand its productive capacity into profitable new lines. That's what his job is all about. He's got to find ideas of the kind you're ready to offer, or he's not going to be running that business very long—not in today's highly competitive market.

Mind you, this doesn't mean he's easy to get to. He may be surrounded by a bristling perimeter of receptionists and secretaries and phone answerers and assorted stooges whom you'll have to fight your way past in order to speak to the great man himself. In one sense that's exactly what they're there for—to make sure his valuable time doesn't get wasted by any weirdos or phonies or ego-trippers or idiots who have nothing more important to do than hear themselves talk.

On the other hand, don't assume, either, that he's necessarily hard to reach. As for screening out phonies, that bristling barrier of secretaries and flunkies may be more camouflage than protection. Often, the smaller the man, the more he likes to surround himself with such trappings of power in order to convince the world (and himself) that he's someone really important, whereas a genuine leader doesn't need that kind of window dressing—he's apt to operate in the simplest kind of setup.

I recall a perfect example of this from my own experience. Several years before the 1980 Olympic Games were to be held in Moscow, a client company I served as a PR adviser and marketing consultant came to me with an unusual problem.

Their parent corporation had joined a three-way consortium aimed at obtaining the merchandising franchise in the United States for the gold medals commemorating the Olympic Games in Moscow. The previous edition, issued by the Canadian government to celebrate the Montreal Olympics, had proved tremendously profitable. There was every reason to believe the Moscow commemorative medals would sell just as well.

Consequently there was apt to be intense bidding for the U.S. sales rights. Because I had formerly represented West Germany and the European Common Market, it was assumed my foreign expertise might be particularly relevant. Did I have any ideas on how to go after the Olympic-medal franchise in Moscow?

The bidders would have to go to Russia and make their pitch in person.

To me the answer was obvious. "Get Armand Hammer to join me in making a presentation in Moscow."

If you've never heard of Armand Hammer, let me tell you that he's one of America's biggest industrial tycoons—a genuine Daddy Warbucks. He's also the one who knows the most about dealing with the Soviets. He has probably initiated and consummated more and larger commercial deals with the Russians than any other businessman alive. Not only would he know the ropes in regard to coping with Kremlin red tape; he would already have the confidence and trust of the Russians because of his previous business dealings with them.

My clients were awestruck at my suggestion. Armand Hammer? Wow, terrific idea. "But what makes you think that big an operator would have the slightest interest in joining us in this kind of a project?" they asked.

My answer was simple: "Because, like every other businessman, he's interested in making money."

"But do you *know* him?" I was asked.

"Who has to know him?" I replied.

To make a long story short, I picked up the telephone, got his number from a banking house I know, and put through a direct call to his home.

The great Armand Hammer answered the phone himself.

I explained why I was calling. He was immediately interested in participating in the project, provided he could have a certain percentage of the franchise. In fifteen minutes we had reached an agreement in principle.

As often as not, that's how difficult it is to present—successfully—a bright idea to a business big shot. The bigger he is, the faster he'll make a decision and give you an answer. It has always paid for him to listen.

This is not to say you'll always find it that easy. If you know someone who can provide you with a personal introduction to Mr. Big, so much the better. By all means, grease the cogwheels and they'll turn that much faster. But if you have no such entrée, here's . . .

RULE NUMBER 2

Don't hesitate to go in cold

In most cases the best procedure is to make contact by telephone, arrange an appointment, then follow up with a face-to-face meeting. This way the meeting is most likely to be productive. You won't have to waste time introducing yourself or explaining the purpose of your visit. He already knows who you are and why you're there. So you can devote all the precious time he's allotting you to socking home your message—to convincing him that he should do whatever you want him to do.

But let's suppose you run into that bristling barrier of secretaries and assistants. How do you get through? Well, try the following:

• *Speak with assurance and authority.* For instance, let's say the head of the company is John Taylor, and we'll call you Lew Martin. When the switchboard operator answers, simply say, "John Taylor, please"—as if the two of you are old buddies and you expect to be put right through. Chances are you will be.

  On the other hand, if you get shuttled from assistant to assistant, just announce yourself to each one: "This is Lew Martin calling John Taylor"—and if they want to know what you're calling about, say "A business matter. I'd prefer to discuss it directly with him if you don't mind."

Sooner or later, of course, a voice (usually female) will say, "Mr. Taylor's office." Again your response might be, "This is Lew Martin calling John Taylor."

At this point, if you're lucky, she *may* turn you right over to him. But more likely she'll put you through a catechism of questions first, in which case . . .

• *Have your answers ready beforehand.* A frequent query she's likely to throw at you is "What company are you with, Mr. Martin?"

Assuming you're on your own, I would suggest replying, "I own my own company," or "I'm an independent consultant" or "I'm a marketing consultant."

Next question: "And what is this call in regard to?"

If it's the boss man's secretary who asks you that, you can't very well sidestep her query. My advice, however, would be to make your reply as terse and tantalizing as possible—terse, tantalizing, and irresistible—for example, "A business proposition aimed at increasing your company's sales volume" or "A way to reduce your production costs" or "A new product line for your company" or "A proposal to expand your marketing area." And "I need only five minutes of his time, and he will be grateful to you for putting me through."

Obviously the exact wording will depend on the nature of the idea you wish to present. But some response like these, designed to pique her boss's curiosity, will give you the best chance of getting through.

However, there's another possible obstacle you must be prepared for. The big shot's secretary may tell you, "Mr. Taylor is not in the office just now" or "Mr. Taylor is in conference" or "Mr. Taylor is talking on another line." It's ten to one she'll add, "Can I take a message?" or "Can someone else help you?" The best way to handle this turn of events is not to let it happen, that is . . .

• *Take the initiative to avoid being sidetracked.* In other words, before she can offer to take a message or turn you over to someone else, cut in briskly with "How soon do you expect him back?" or "When would be a good time to reach him?"

Then, when she gives you this information, thank her and hang up promptly. A bonus in this event is that when you do phone back at the time she suggests, she'll probably remember you and feel obliged to make sure you do get a chance to talk to Mr. Big this time.

A somewhat trickier situation is when the secretary offers to take your name and number and have her boss call you when he's free. Although she may suggest this in perfectly good faith, don't hold your breath waiting for him to do so. Phone memos can easily get mislaid or overlooked; besides which, her jotted notation may only hazily convey the gist of what you told her. And if he's got a busy schedule, it's human nature for him to shrug off your call with the thought, "If it's anything important, the guy'll get back to me."

Probably the simplest way to avoid this frustrating sand trap is to tell her you'll be going out shortly; therefore, to avoid missing his call, you would prefer to phone back yourself.

Summing up everything I've just said on how to get through to the head honcho is . . .

RULE NUMBER 3

Plan your telephone strategy
beforehand, and know exactly
what you're going to say

Now, then, no matter how well you handle your telephone approach, the boss man's secretary may still come back after telling him you're on the line and say, "Mr. Taylor suggests that you write him a letter explaining what you have in mind, and then if he's interested, he'll get in touch with you."

Well, there's not much you can do in that case except to go ahead and write the letter—and hope you write it well enough so that he *will* want to get in touch. However, there may also be times when you yourself will decide to write a preliminary letter *before* making your telephone approach.

Basically there are two possible reasons for choosing this way: (1) Your proposal may require too much explanation and buildup to be put across in a brief oral presentation, or (2) Your idea may be so drastically new and different and innovative that your listener is likely to have trouble absorbing and adjusting to such a far-out concept in, say, a mere fifteen-minute meeting. That is, he may understand what you're telling him and even find your logic persuasive, yet also find it so startling that he won't trust his own judgment till he's had time to digest and mull over everything you've said.

Here's an example that was told to me by a lawyer friend. He had recently been called on to settle the estate of a deceased client. Just before he died, this client had sunk a good deal of money into a new business venture. The venture was now at a critical phase and needed another hefty infusion of capital. It was certain that the venture would pay off big in due time, probably within a year. Yet without this additional investment right away, the enterprise was likely to fail, or else would have to be liquidated immediately at a loss of thousands of dollars to the estate.

The client's major asset was a sizable hunk of stock in a small, highly specialized machine-tool company. By selling this stock the estate could raise the needed capital. What's more, the lawyer had a bright idea about where to find a buyer quick—someone who was ready to pay a generous price.

There was just one catch. The machine-tool firm was a family-owned corporation. It had been founded by four brothers at the turn of the century, but since then the stock had passed through inheritance into the possession of more than twenty different relatives scattered all over; in fact three of them were living and working in other parts of the world. Yet according to the terms of the charter, no shares could be sold to outside individuals without the unanimous consent of all the family stockholders. To get such consent might take months.

Nevertheless, the lawyer knew he had a good idea and decided to broach it to the president of the company. The prospective buyer was a talented design engineer and production genius whom the company had actually tried to hire two years earlier. He had turned down their employment offer because it didn't include a stock option. Now, however, given a chance to buy into the firm, he was eager and willing to join the machine-tool company—and his engineering and executive talents were sure to prove major assets. His presence would automatically boost the firm's competitive position in the industry, increase its sales potential, and give its business rating a shot in the arm.

On the other hand, the president was an ultraconservative type. To negotiate the deal he would have to invoke an emergency clause in the company's charter, enabling him to override the unanimous-consent requirement. By doing so he was apt to anger at least some of the stockholders and maybe jeopardize his own continued position as head of the firm.

What would you have done in the lawyer's place? I think it's a safe bet you wouldn't just lift the phone, make an appointment, then show up and try to fast-talk the president into going along with your idea in a brief face-to-face meeting. His off-the-cuff response would almost certainly be negative.

What the lawyer actually did was write a letter first, carefully outlining all aspects of the proposed stock sale. Then he waited for the facts to sink in, allowing the president time to get over his initial shock and outrage and get used to the mind-boggling notion of violating the eighty-year-old family-ownership tradition. When the lawyer finally did arrange a face-to-face meeting, he was able to drive home all his points on well-prepared factual grounds.

The president may have been conservative, but he was no fool. Facts were facts, and the potential benefits were too important to pass up. The lawyer got an okay for the stock sale, the deceased client's estate got the capital needed to protect his earlier investment, and the machine-tool company got a talented new engineer and executive who, in little more than two years, has increased its profits and is already seen as its future chief executive.

Here's a more down-to-earth example. A local builder, whom I'll call Al Rizzoli, was worried about his standing in the community. As his business took a nose dive he shifted course and laid plans to open a hamburger drive-in. Many, if not most, of his customers would be teenagers, so he wanted to publicize the opening with a flashy publicity gimmick aimed at that age group. At the same time, he also wanted to worm his way back into the graces of the older, more uptight segment of the community, especially since they weren't too happy about his hamburger drive-in plans to begin with.

The gimmick he dreamed up was a teenage beauty contest, featuring nubile, bikini-clad high-school nymphets. Yet, with amazing nerve, he proposed to have the contest not only sponsored by the Ladies University Club but also held in their clubhouse auditorium. The club, I might add, was composed of local society dames, mostly in their fifties and sixties—none of them favorably disposed toward sexy displays of youthful female flesh.

Sound crazy? Everyone thought so when Rizzoli first announced his brilliant idea. Had he simply phoned the club's Madam President for a chance to address the members, then barged in and bluntly asked them to sponsor his beauty contest, he would doubtless have been hissed off the platform before he even got a chance to finish.

Instead, Al Rizzoli first wrote a dignified letter to the Ladies University Club explaining how he would return their esteemed favor if they would graciously grant it. His contracting company would perform, free of charge, the estimated six thousand dollars' worth of fix-up work needed to restore the Victorian clubhouse to prime condition. Also, he would personally match, dollar for dollar, the scholarship fund raised by the club's secondhand-book sale and rummage sale. And the scholarship winners would share the spotlight with the beauty-contest winners at the opening of his drive-in.

To quote a line from *The Godfather*, it was "an offer they couldn't refuse." Once his generous proposal had time to work its irresistible charm on the minds of the august society ladies, they felt they practically had to accept. This leads us to . . .

RULE NUMBER 4

To put across a drastically new or radical idea,
lay the groundwork by letter
before making your pitch in person

Let's take time out right here to talk about what kind of letter you should write. Nobody can teach you how to write well in one easy lesson. But I can almost guarantee that you will turn out an effective letter if you follow these seven rules:

1. *Write simply.* Many people, when they have to put down thoughts on paper, are seized by an urge to become pompous and dignified—the way policemen, when interviewed by reporters on TV, start talking about "apprehending the perpetrators." They have the odd notion that this makes them sound more important and impressive. Believe me, nothing could be further from the truth. Take my word for it that the more you can make your writing sound like ordinary, everyday speech, the more effective it will be.

2. *Write briefly.* The fewer the words in a sentence, the better the sentence. The fewer the number of sentences in a paragraph, the better the paragraph. The fewer the paragraphs, the better the letter.

No matter how well educated a person may be, the mind is inherently lazy. As a result, everyone—most especially a harried businessman whose time is valuable—would rather read a short, crisp business letter than a long, involved one. Also, he will put down your letter with a much better idea of what you want if you make your pitch as brief as possible. So keep it short. Say exactly what you want to say, and not one word more.

3. *Write clearly.* This is actually one of the hardest things in the world to do. Unless you're a born literary genius, you'll probably have to write, rewrite, then tear your letter apart and rewrite it all over again. When you're done, have somebody read the letter cold, then make him repeat back to you in his own words the gist of what you were trying to say. If he can't, you haven't written clearly enough and you'd better start all over.

Clarity is closely related to brevity. Many people think

that the more words you pile on, the clearer your point will become. Actually it works just the other way. Too many words act like a smoke screen. They don't bring out your meaning; they fog it up.

4. *Write from your reader's viewpoint.* Don't fill your letter with *I*'s and *me*'s—fill it with *you*'s. You yourself are already convinced that your idea's a winner. Now you're trying to convince *him*. To do that, the main thing you have to emphasize is what's in it for him.

5. *Write logically.* By this I mean, arrange your thoughts sensibly so that one point leads to the next, and on to the next, and so on. Basically it's a matter of organization. You start from the reader's position and his point of view, and try to lead him, step by step, to your position and your point of view.

I generally use three rules of thumb in organizing a letter. In my first sentence (or sentences) I state as succinctly as possible the proposition I wish to make to the person who'll receive my letter—always emphasizing what's in it for him. In other words, I get to the point immediately and dangle the bait up front.

Next I tell him, again as succinctly as possible, who *I* am and why *I'm* broaching this idea to him, in other words, I tell him frankly where my selfish interest lies. In the vernacular, I let him know "where I'm coming from."

The body of the letter, from here on, will be mostly an expansion and further explanation of my idea.

Lastly I keep in mind what I want the letter to accomplish—what I hope will happen as a result of my writing it—and use that for my closing paragraph. As a rule, and in the context of this chapter, the purpose of my letter is to bring about a face-to-face meeting. So that's what I end by requesting.

6. *Write correctly.* If you're not sure about grammar and spelling and punctuation, have someone check your letter

from this standpoint. There's bound to be someone in reach who can do so—maybe a local schoolteacher. A word of caution, however. If you ask one to correct your grammar, spelling, and punctuation, and he ventures beyond this and tries to inflict his own ideas on you or volunteers to rewrite your letter, beware. You'll probably be safer sticking to your own version.

7. *Make your letter pleasing to the eye.* A small investment in letterhead stationery is often worthwhile. It tends to make the reader of your letter take you more seriously and see you as someone who's already established in the business world. But a clean white sheet of bond paper and a crisp new envelope will do.

However, I don't think there's any excuse for sending out a business letter that's handwritten. You must know *someone* who's taken typing in high school or has worked as a typist. If not, look for a typist's ad in your local newspaper or on the bulletin board at your supermarket. As a last resort, ask the proprietor of your local typewriter store for a name. Remember, until you meet the person you're contacting, fact to face, *your letter represents you.* And you want to make the best possible impression, don't you?

Let's say you finally got through to Mr. Big on the telephone. You explained to him in a few well-chosen sentences why it would pay him to see you and hear your idea, and a meeting was set up. At long last, then, his secretary has just ushered you into his office, and now it's time to make your pitch and turn him on.

What to do?

I'll tell you one thing *not* to do, and that is wait until the very moment you're standing there with your mouth open before figuring out what you're going to say. This is something you should have thought about and decided long before you got out of bed that morning.

Your basic *luck-making idea* should be crystal clear in your mind. How to *present* your idea should be equally clear. You've probably worked it out almost sentence by sentence and then practiced in front of a mirror—maybe even tried it out on a friend or someone in your family.

Don't worry about all this making you too rote perfect and mechanical. You weren't practicing to memorize lines, anyway. The purpose was to get you thoroughly familiar with the logic and sense of what you're going to tell him.

Also, don't worry about your mind going blank from stage fright. A good technique is to jot down your main points in numerical order on a small card. Carry this in your pocket when you keep your appointment with Mr. Big and don't hesitate to glance at it from time to time whenever you wish to refresh your memory.

Think how much time actors spend rehearsing a role before they actually face an audience—all this in order to polish their lines and help them deliver the most powerful performance of which they're capable.

You, too, want to stage the most powerful possible performance when you make your pitch to Mr. Big. So be sure to heed . . .

RULE NUMBER 5

Rehearse your presentation

If there's one crucial factor that can make the difference between putting your idea across and having it brushed off, that factor is *your own enthusiasm.*

If you yourself believe in the idea and *know* it will work, then you'll have no trouble remembering your presentation and convincing your listener(s). If you aren't wholly convinced, you shouldn't be presenting it in the first place.

Remember that conviction and enthusiasm are *contagious.* The surest way to make Mr. Big share your enthusiasm is not by any cold, analytical, step-by-step reasoning process. The quickest, surest way is simply to let him catch it from you.

So to sell your idea successfully, always bear in mind . . .

RULE NUMBER 6

You've gotta believe

You recall that in discussing how to compose the most effective letter I urged you to tell the person you're writing to, as soon as possible, what's in it for him—or, in other words dangle the bait up front. This is even more important when you present your idea in person. It's actually the secret of all sales success—namely, to make the other party *want* what you have to offer.

And the simplest way to accomplish this, of course, is to show him how your idea will benefit *him.*

Once you've firmly implanted this fact in his mind, you've got him hooked. From that moment on he'll be as eager to turn your idea into reality as you are. The remainder of your task will simply be to show him that the idea is practical and workable, and then give the details of what must be done to bring it about.

The moment when your listener absorbs this *self-motivation* can be intensely dramatic—especially when you've put across your message with a few high-impact words.

In this connection, I remember an incident that occurred when I was developing my computerized astrology business. As I mentioned in an earlier chapter, I traveled all over the world, seeing how astrology was practiced in different countries and looking up the experts who were considered by other astrologers to be the leaders in their field.

One such person was a woman in London, widely regarded as one of the world's greatest astrologers. Because of this, plus the fact that she spoke English, I felt she might be an excellent choice to work with in developing a computer program that could cast horoscopes automatically.

But when I called on her at her address in London, her attitude at first seemed to douse cold water on my hopes. As I arrived she was just about to leave her apartment, and showed little if any interest in hearing what I had to say.

"Young man," she informed me severely, "I'm due at the BBC to record a radio program on astrology. If you can tell me in five minutes what you want to see me about, I'll stay and listen—otherwise I'm afraid you'll have to come back some other time.

I said, "I can tell you in less than one minute. I've come all the way over here from the United States to make you a business offer. It'll require you to work your head off for about the next six months—but after that the chances are you'll never have to work another day for the rest of your life. If that interests you, I'll go on talking. If not, I'll leave right now and not bother you again."

The astrologer stared at me for a moment. Then she stepped back from the door and started taking off her hat and coat, saying, "Come in."

This story neatly illustrates . . .

RULE NUMBER 7

Tempt your listener by showing what your idea
can do for him personally

There are times, however, when the success of your idea may be threatened by a snag that develops in a totally unexpected quarter.

Earlier, for instance, I told you how I developed and carried through a project by which French-model tanks would be manufactured in the United States at an American foundry. This enormous undertaking took me two years and required countless trips abroad to persuade the member companies of the French consortium to let us manufacture their tank model over here in exchange for the spare-parts business, which would amount to 30 percent of the total program. I also had to line up five foreign countries to buy the tanks.

At last all the parts of the project were put together. I had broken a leg coming down an escalator at Orly Airport near Paris on my way home. I had to get up from a hospital bed with one leg in a clumsy cast in order to return to France to participate in the signing of the complicated multinational contract. The U.S. Treasury Department was ecstatic: This one program in itself would go a long way toward correcting our balance-of-trade deficit.

Suddenly the Pentagon threw a monkey wrench into the whole deal. Rather than let the French invade their military turf, the U.S. Army insisted on developing a similar tank of their own design, and at tremendous cost to the American taxpayer. I call this type of blind, stubborn opposition the "NIH Syndrome," for "Not Invented Here." My client later sold the plant and the contract to Lockheed.

On a miniature scale, a friend of mine had a similar experience in New York City. A new magazine had become terrifically popular almost overnight. He approached the company's head man—in this case the publisher—with an idea for developing a syndicated newspaper feature based on the weekly contents of the magazine. He was invited to come in for a meeting and explain his proposal.

The meeting went splendidly. The publisher liked the idea and was willing to put up money to develop a pilot sample of the proposed feature. But for some odd reason one of the magazine executives seemed to radiate silent hostility to the whole project. This was the sales-promotion director whom I'll call Fred Jarman. My friend was puzzled, since he had never met the man before.

Just as the meeting was about to end Jarman asked that the preparation of the sample feature be delayed. A new promotional program was getting under way, he explained, and he wanted time to see how the feature would fit into the program.

This ploy seemed an obvious stall. My friend went away mystified. What did Jarman have against him and the newspaper-feature project, which offered obvious benefits, both financial and promotional, to the magazine?

Suddenly the explanation hit him. Here was another example of the NIH Syndrome. Promotional ideas like the newspaper feature were supposed to come from Jarman himself, not from outsiders. As it turned out, Jarman eventually succeeded in having the project permanently derailed.

In such cases there are two tacks you can take. One is to persuade your opponent that you pose no threat, that you're willing to proceed under his aegis and let him take credit for your idea. The other is to assess the relative strength of your support and opposition inside the company, and if you think your side packs enough clout to win, then square off for a fight, open or covert.

In any event, my advice is . . .

RULE NUMBER 8

Be prepared for unforeseen
challenges to your idea

Here's an important thought to keep in mind when pitching a new idea. It can help to dispel your doubts and increase your confidence. If your idea was soundly thought out in the first place, the project will soon take on a life of its own. It will tend to succeed no matter how well or how badly you present your idea.

I first got clued in on this years ago by a veteran door-to-door salesman. "You soon learn not to be put off by individual turndowns," he told me. "No matter how good or bad a salesman you are, you can always rely on the law of averages. That is, if you ring a hundred doorbells, you're sure to make at least X number of sales. And you'll get that many in good weather, bad weather, sick, healthy, no matter how you feel or what kind of day it is. All you have to do is keep walking and keep ringing."

The same principle is utilized by companies that specialize in selling housewares by home demonstration. Such companies draw their sales staffs from all walks of life, some recruits being natural-born salesmen, others incurable oafs. But even the oafs can be taught to produce their share of hits. By setting up the demonstrations through a centralized prospecting system and teaching their salesmen a tested, foolproof demonstration routine, the companies ensure a constant flow of orders. They know by statistical results that the routine will work at least X percent of the time.

You, too, can be confident that your idea is part way to success before you even walk into Mr. Big's office. Just remember . . .

RULE NUMBER 9

Built-in success forces are at work
from the moment you get a luck-making idea
and start doing something about it

One last word to the wise. The moment you see that Mr. Big likes your idea, *stop selling.* You've scored—your job's done. Answer any further questions he may ask, by all means. Provide any additional information he may require. But stop selling and leave as quickly as you can. In short, follow . . .

RULE NUMBER 10

Once you've sold a person on your idea,
leave well enough alone—
don't *un*sell him

At this moment you stand as high in his favor as you ever will. From here on you have nowhere to go but *down*. And that's exactly where you *will* go if you sit around gilding the lily and piling on unnecessary details. You've accomplished exactly what you came for, so don't spoil it. More deals are lost by overselling than you realize.

12

Your Secret Power Network

Do you remember a chain of events that I described to you a couple of chapters back, concerning the monthly medical newsletter that I publish?

I told you about a visit to my printer, and how he put me in touch by phone with someone who could help me find a brand-new sales outlet for my newsletter. I followed up by meeting that person face to face, and as a result of our meeting he recommended my newsletter to the mail-order house he worked for.

Meanwhile, a syndicator I'd approached earlier *also* recommended my newsletter to that same mail-order house, just on the strength of our past business contacts. This brought me an invitation from the mail-order house to present my newsletter personally for their consideration.

That same syndicator had, himself, previously turned down my newsletter because he was already handling a similar publication for an oil company. But when that publication failed, he recommended my newsletter as a substitute. When I followed up on this new lead, the oil company not only showed interest in distributing my medical newsletter, it also broached the idea of my producing a gourmet newsletter for them as well.

In other words, a wide chain of contacts had opened up three possible business deals—two involving new sales outlets for my medical newsletter and a third based on a proposal that I begin publishing another type of newsletter as well.

Notice that two of my contacts—the printer and the syndicator—were long-time acquaintances. The others were brand new. I had started the chain of events on my own initiative. But once things were set in motion, further developments began happening of their own accord.

The recommendations by the syndicator, the invitation from the mail-order house, the oil company's suggestion that I produce a gourmet newsletter for them—all these occurred spontaneously, without any fresh effort on my part.

If I seem to dwell overemphatically on this situation, it's not just to bloat my ego. It's to illustrate an important luck-making concept that I call my *secret power network*.

I've already used the network analogy to get across the idea of a complete flow of business energy. That is, you start out with an *idea* for a product or service, then, by making various *contacts*, you begin turning your idea into reality, thus you eventually *make your own luck* by completing the energy *circuit* when your product or service reaches the consumer.

This is the basic luck-making process.

But now, when I speak of my secret power network, I'm adding a whole new dimension of meaning to the term "network." In fact, I'm about to introduce you to a technique and a resource that can literally transform your whole career.

If you carry away nothing else from my book, let it be this one concept—the *power-network principle*.

I guarantee you it can increase your earning power, upgrade your business status, generate luck that you're not even expecting, and permanently enrich your whole life.

Sounds too miraculous to be true?

Well, believe me it *is* true. And you can prove it to yourself by trying out this principle in your own life—preferably starting today. You'll find it's like money invested in a growing business or a seed planted in fertile soil because it tends to flourish and send out profitable new shoots in all directions.

Now, just what is this secret power-network principle that I'm making such a big deal of?

Let me give you a simple example.

Janet Forsman is a highly successful realtor in my community. Yet, on first meeting her, you might never guess she is such a crackerjack businesswoman. She certainly doesn't come on as a high-pressure sales type or hustler, in either manner or appearance. On the contrary, she's a rather motherly little woman who seems to have all the time in the world to chat with anyone she meets.

And therein lies her secret.

Let's say she runs into a friend on the street and that friend introduces her to someone she's never met before—a guy named Walt Green.

Janet could politely shake hands with him, utter a few meaningless words, then turn back to her friend and swap a few personal news items before saying good-bye and walking on. Chances are, she and Walt Green might never lay eyes on each other again—or, if they did, they might not even recognize each other.

But Janet doesn't operate that way. She's a warmhearted, friendly woman who enjoys meeting people, who has a normal share of inquisitiveness, and who is never too busy to talk—or *listen*.

With a few brief, chatty conversational ploys, she'll soon have Walt Green gabbing away as if they were old friends, in fact, telling her his life story. And not to any cold-blooded, mercenary audience, either. Janet's genuinely interested in other human beings. When she asks Walt Green a question, it's because she really wants to know the answer. At the same time, her busy eyes and brain and feminine intuition are registering all sorts of data about him.

Has his company just transferred him here? Is he likely to move away soon or retire? Are his children growing up and starting out on their own, leaving him and his wife with no need for their present size home? Is this fellow a go-getter with upward mobility, who may soon be in the market for a larger, more expensive house? Might he be interested in a small vacation home, which could also serve as a safe and profitable investment?

By the time the conversation is over—even if the encounter lasted just a few minutes—Janet will have accumulated a whole dossier of information about Walt Green.

Sooner or later she'll be back in touch with him—by note or phone call or postcard. And if ever he has a property to put on the market or is looking to buy one himself, where is he likely to turn first? Janet Forsman will already be firmly fixed in his mind—not only as a realtor but as a friend who's personally aware of his life situation and needs.

Mind you, I'm not advocating that you *pretend* to like people or be interested in them just out of mercenary motives, though there are plenty of success hunters who operate just that cold-bloodedly. On the contrary, if someone turns you off or puts your back up, I'd advise you to leave him alone. It's not likely you could ever establish a rewarding relationship with that person, anyhow.

But the fact is—if you'll take off your blinkers and

open up your mind and ears and, yes, your heart—you'll find that most human beings are really quite interesting critters.

Once we come out of our tight little shells and stop being totally absorbed in our own petty self-importance, the great outside world and the whole human race become a good deal more interesting. This is why so many people (and not only bored housewives) become addicted to watching television soap operas. Other people's private lives and personal problems are endlessly fascinating once we really tune in on them.

Quiz

Stop right here and ask yourself:

- Did I discover something new about any other person today?
- Did I especially notice anything about my associates today?
- Did I make a new acquaintance today?
- Did I learn anything useful or interesting from anyone today?
- Can I remember exactly what any other person (who's not an attractive member of the opposite sex) was wearing today?

If your answer to all these questions is No, then you probably need to sensitize yourself more to other people.

As you'll learn presently, this is an important requirement or first step in developing your own secret power network.

Let's go back to that successful realtor, Janet Forsman. Janet's been in the real estate business in our community for almost twenty years. By now she must have met and filed away mental data on hundreds of people like Walt Green—or, more likely, thousands, since she belongs to various clubs and attends a good many social functions.

These contacts make up her secret power network. Not all of them have, or will ever, become actual customers of hers. Yet to Janet each one represents a potential real estate transaction.

And even those who will never buy or rent a house through her or bring her a property to dispose of may still recommend her services to their friends and neighbors. Janet is that kind of person. Because she takes an interest in people, they respond by taking an interest in her.

All businessmen need their own particular kind of power network. That's why they form such organizations as Kiwanis and Lions and local booster clubs. Ditto for professional people such as doctors, lawyers, engineers, and indeed any other group big enough to form its own society or association. On Long Island, for instance, there's a group of cartoonists who get together for lunch once a month to trade shop talk.

I know a young man who for several years worked as a salesclerk in a local camera shop. Being courteous and patient and intelligent, as well as a skilled photographer himself, with a thorough knowledge of photographic equipment, he soon built up a loyal circle of customers—many of whom became not just customers but personal friends.

Eventually this young man grew dissatisfied with the commissions he was being paid at the camera store, so he switched to a more promising job as a clothing salesman at a menswear shop down the street. Not surprisingly, many of his former photography customers now became his clothing customers. In effect, he had built up his own private power network.

You, too, as an independent luck maker and wheeler-dealer, need your own private power network. And because you're on your own, you must—like Janet Forsman and that young camera and clothing salesman I just mentioned—build the network yourself.

But first, before we talk about that, let's try to be a little clearer about exactly what I mean by a secret power network.

In Janet's case her network consists primarily of *potential clients*. In the case of the young salesclerk, his network consists of *satisfied customers*.

When it comes to professional societies or luncheon clubs, such as the one I mentioned on Long Island, they're composed of peer groups—that is to say, a network of *fellow workers* in the same field who meet to exchange useful information, such as tips on trends or new craft techniques or how to deal with problems shared by all members of the group.

Trade magazines and professional journals are a way of extending this network statewide or nationally through the articles, news items, and advertisements they contain.

Businessmen's get-togethers tend to be more general, in that they include merchants in various lines of retailing, skilled tradesmen, bankers, operators of various kinds of service establishments. Yet they also tend to be more *local*, insofar as the members all live or work in the same community.

Important note: Ethnic groups often provide useful power networks—not just for business deals inside the group but also for luck-making connections to a wider market.

A good example of this is the career of a friend of mine, Johnny Szymanski.

Johnny grew up in a Polish enclave of Detroit, called Hamtramck. He was ambitious to become a newspaper reporter, but he had no college education in journalism or any kind of practical journalistic experience. In those days his ethnic background was hardly an ideal qualification for any sort of writing career—let alone the fact that the Great Depression was on and few jobs were available on newspapers or anywhere else. His prospects seemed hopeless.

Yet there were certain facts in Johnny's favor. His neighbors bought Detroit newspapers and wanted to read about local doings in Hamtramck as well as in other parts of the city. And newspaper editors wanted to reach that particular segment of their audience. Johnny knew his community intimately and spoke all the Slavic languages—Polish, Russian, Ukrainian, Slovak, Czech. He was an insider compared to any ordinary reporter who might venture from the city room into the blue-collar wilds of Hamtramck.

He talked the city editor of the morning paper into taking him on as a local stringer at space rates of so much per column inch. From there he soon graduated into wider reporting and went on to a successful business career in public relations and sales promotion.

Thus, Johnny Szymanski used his ethnic connections as a power network in two ways: The network not only provided him with *sources of news* from inside the community, it also gave him a *salable commodity* with which to make his own luck in the outside world.

What have we learned, if anything, from the foregoing case histories?

First of all, let's define a power network as a widespread web of friends and acquaintances who can help you make your own luck.

They can help you make your own luck in three ways:

1. *A power network can provide you with valuable information,* just as the CIA might set up an intelligence network to gather and feed back information from a foreign country.

For example, one of those cartoonists I mentioned on Long Island was recently approached by a West Coast newspaper syndicate. The syndicate offered him a contract to draw a famous old comic strip, replacing an artist who was about to retire. The cartoonist declined but mentioned the offer to his luncheon buddies. One was very much interested. He phoned the syndicate that same day and wound up getting the job.

Information of this sort is swapped at every meeting. Not long before the incident I've just described, one luncher brought news that the cartoon editor of *Playboy* was looking for material. Another member of the group promptly submitted a comic feature. It was accepted and now appears frequently in the "Playboy Funnies" section of the magazine.

Another example is Dr. Bruce Frome, a Los Angeles anesthesiologist whose energy and enthusiasm have prodded him into all sorts of ventures besides the practice of medicine. His cousin, Alan Frome, is well aware of the doctor's keen interest in new business enterprises and often acts as an informal scout—thus, in effect, becoming part of Dr. Frome's power network.

Recently, while visiting Toronto, Alan was startled to see some machinery in a camera shop that could process a roll of color film in only thirty-two minutes. He phoned the Japanese company that made the machinery and learned they were setting up a new plant in California, so he flew there to give his cousin Bruce the hot news.

Dr. Frome was so impressed when he checked out the machines that he immediately bought one for $150,000. In March 1980, in Encino, a suburb of Los Angeles, he opened his first One Hour Photo Developing Center. It can process and deliver quality prints from 110-, 126-, and 135-mm color film in one hour at twenty-nine cents per print.

The store proved so successful that he now has three stores in the Los Angeles area and expects to have half a dozen more in operation before the end of the year. He also plans to extend the business to Honolulu, and is now selling franchises that may soon lead to the opening of more such stores all over the country.

These exciting developments have all taken place within a year—as a result of information received from just one member of Dr. Frome's private power network.

2. *A power network can stimulate luck-making contacts and opportunities.* Usually this will come about through phone calls or people getting in touch with you in other ways, such as by letter or a doorbell ring. When asked how they happened to obtain your name, almost invariably they will reply that So-and-So told them about you.

For instance, Fay Ruthven is a housewife with a keen interest in photography. At first it was mostly a hobby, although she practiced it as an art and had had several local exhibits of her work.

One day a friend who loves cats and dogs, and is a volunteer worker at the local animal shelter, asked Fay for a favor. Each week the shelter placed an ad in the local paper, describing one of their animals that was waiting for adoption. Each ad would feature a picture of the animal—usually an amateurish snap by one of the staff. However, the woman who had been doing this had just moved to Florida, so the volunteer wanted Fay to take over the chore.

It sounded like an interesting challenge, so Fay agreed. With her usual artistic intent, she made every picture as attractive and appealing as possible. The number of adoptions quickly picked up. One day Fay got an unexpected telephone call asking her to take some photographs of the caller's Yorkshire terrier. It turned out the woman had noticed the pictures in the animal shelter's newspaper ads, and one of the volunteer workers had told her about Fay's work.

Fay accepted the assignment, and the woman was so pleased with the results that other calls soon followed. The Yorkie, it seems, was a show dog, and his owner's enthusiasm had spread to other members of her dog club. Each new client became a cheerleading member of Fay's power network, along with cat owners, who were equally eager for her work.

The proprietor of a local pet store hired Fay to provide a weekly photographic blowup for display in his shop window.

The supreme accolade came when a top local portrait photographer began to exhibit her work in his own window—and then shot pet-portrait orders her way for a 25 percent commission. Fay's reputation—and income—are growing steadily and she now has all the work she can handle.

3. *A power network can develop into profitable business relationships.* In this case the members of the network themselves become your customers or agents.

An example is Bob Lubek, the son of one of our neighbors. He's now studying mechanical engineering at a local college, but when we first moved here, he was still a teenage hot-rodder—and a hustler from the word go. Bob was such an expert mechanic that he made a regular business of buying and repairing secondhand jalopies, then selling them at a markup to his high-school buddies.

Working alone, with limited operating capital, this was a rather slow business. Even so, Bob would usually have two or three cars in various stages of repair cluttering his family's driveway. And friends would often borrow one overnight or on weekends for a date.

Gradually it dawned on Bob that he was concentrating on the wrong operation. He realized he could make far more money on used-car rentals than he could on resales. In effect, he became an early exponent of the rent-a-wreck business, which is now becoming a nationwide trend. Instead of lending his cars for a day or two, he would rent them to classmates who were "in between" cars of their own or who hadn't yet accumulated enough money from their stock-boy or gas-station jobs to make their first used-car purchase.

When Bob graduated from high school, some of his closest buddies (who were car nuts like himself) took full-time jobs as body-shop repairmen and garage mechanics. Bob himself was headed for college but saw no reason to give up his profitable car-rental business.

In effect, his mechanic buddies now became his power network.

When a car comes in for repairs and is likely to be in the shop all day or longer, the mechanic will ask the owner if he's interested in cheap temporary transportation while his car is being fixed. At least half the owners say yes—especially when they hear that a dependable, if not flashy-looking, car can by rented for under ten dollars a day and only a few cents a mile.

Bob's ambition is to become an automotive engineer and car stylist. But meanwhile he's already a successful small-business man and is putting himself through college with five rebuilt cars as his operating equipment. On any given day of the week he rarely has fewer than three of them rented out to repair-shop customers, and usually one or more rented to a friend or neighbor.

So far he hasn't found it necessary to advertise because his private power network brings him all the business he can handle.

* * *

How can you develop your own power network?

Recently I was asked that same question at a business seminar. I responded with a question of my own: "What business are you in?"

"The furniture business," he replied.

I said, "*Wrong*. You're in the *people* business. The furniture is just incidental."

At first his only reaction was a puzzled stare. I imagine he thought I was trying to be cute or phonily profound or quotably epigrammatic. Or maybe he wasn't even sure I was serious.

But then, as he thought it over, the expression on his face changed completely. "By gosh, you know you're right about that," he muttered in an awed whisper.

And of course I am—take my word for it—though I certainly don't claim to be the first person to arrive at this crucial understanding.

All business, you see, from the very earliest barter exchange to the first trading voyages by merchant seamen is based on personal relationships.

To the extent that such exchanges were not just fleeting contacts but satisfied both parties and therefore might lead to further exchanges in the future, the principle of repeat business was discovered—and society had taken a tremendous step forward.

To the extent that both parties came to know and trust each other, perhaps even like each other a bit, civilization itself was born.

The whole purpose of a business deal, in fact, is to enable people to satisfy their needs. The goods they swap or barter are only means to that end. If they don't achieve satisfaction, the deal was unsuccessful.

In the case of the furniture dealer at the seminar, let's imagine him serving a couple of customers, a man and wife who have walked into the store to buy a replacement for their battered sofa.

In the dealer's eyes he would merely be selling them a piece of furniture.

In my eyes, he would be helping them make their living room more beautiful and comfortable.

If he is able to do so at a fair price and send them away happy—and if he makes such considerations a yardstick for all future transactions in his store—I can practically guarantee that that dealer will find himself running a prosperous and successful business.

Exactly the same principle governs power networks. To build a successful power network, your prime consideration in all contacts and business dealings must be to serve people as well as you can. So get in the habit of reflecting frequently on . . .

THOUGHT NUMBER 1

Power networks are composed of people,
more people
and nothing but people—
therefore people are
your most important resource

Obviously, if people are your most important resource, it will be worth your while to meet as many of them as you can. It's like investing more capital in your business in order to expand your plant and marketing facilities. The more people you know, the bigger your business can be.

One way to do this, of course, is to get out and join clubs and engage in all the social activities you can.

But let me emphasize as strongly as possible—especially if you're shy and tend to be uncomfortable in social groups—that this is not the only way. Often it's not even the best way. Sometimes a one-on-one encounter begun on the street or at a newsstand, or while seated side by side in a waiting room or on an airline flight, may prove the start of a long and enduring friendship.

In fact, the meeting need not even be face to face; it may take place at opposite ends of a telephone line. I know of one such case personally. Both parties are members of the academic profession. At the time of their first contact, one was teaching at a university in Michigan, the other in Georgia.

Over the years, both have moved around frequently yet never lost touch by phone or letter. One now lives in Connecticut, the other in New Jersey. Both have been importantly helpful and influential in each other's career. One even owes an academic appointment to an introduction and recommendation by the other. I know all this through having met and talked to both of them.

It's now nearly twenty-five years—almost a quarter of a century—since they first made contact. And each considers the other one of his closest friends. Yet they still have never met face to face.

So anytime you're feeling discouraged or depressed over your limited opportunities, just bear in mind . . .

THOUGHT NUMBER 2

The more people I get to know, the more effective
my power network will be and the wider
my career horizons will expand

It's startling to realize how often we meet people—and by "meet" I mean be introduced to and speak to—whom we never see again. As the old saying goes, when people come into contact this way, they're like ships that pass in the night. Their faces and names barely register on each other's consciousness.

Memory-training courses are designed to correct this. They teach you trick ways to fix a certain name in your mind, and how to hook up a particular name with a particular face. This is all to the good, no doubt. But it seems to me to miss the real point.

What good are a name and a face if there's nothing attached to them? They're like a label on an empty bottle. Would you carefully save and file an envelope and throw away the message inside?

What matters is the person himself or herself.

Recently I had to get an air conditioner repaired. This unit has given me terrific service, although it's fifteen years old and a now-obsolete model no longer being manufactured. In order to fix it, the repairman had to go to considerable trouble in locating a replacement part.

Despite his rather humdrum job, this guy is one of the jolliest, warmest persons you'd ever care to meet. I happened to be in his shop while he was tracking down the part over the phone.

The manufacturer's order department told him to call a certain plant in Indiana and ask for a Miss Peotter. He did and in two minutes they were gabbing away like old friends. This call was costing him money, mind you, but he took time to mention that one of his kids had a teacher named Mrs. Peotter, and since the name was rather unusual, he wondered if the two might be related. Apparently Miss Peotter asked if the teacher's name was spelled with an "e" or an "i." He in turn inquired about her family's original nationality, commenting that the name sounded vaguely Russian—which, so far as I could follow the conversation, led to her telling him how they had moved from somewhere in the East to their present location in Indiana.

When he hung up, I could only stare in admiration. He may or may not ever have to call that company again, but if he does, you can be darn sure Miss Peotter will remember him and give him special attention. In the present instance, the replacement part he wanted was shipped out, special delivery, that same day.

Mind you, I'm not advocating that you go through this sort of chummy routine every time you come into contact with someone you haven't met. But don't behave as if the two of you are mindless mechanical robots, either. Come alive. Pay attention. Give the other person a chance to register in your mind as a unique human being. Try to get his or her name straight. And when the introduction's over, try to come away from the encounter with a distinct face and a distinct individual registered in your mind.

Remember, there's no point in rushing around to business lunches and social functions and glad-handing everyone in sight if they're all going to slip from your memory like minnows through a net. So here's another thought . . .

THOUGHT NUMBER 3

In building up your power network,
it's not the quantity but the quality
of your relationships that counts

If you had to read through a ten-page report full of boring statistics, you might not remember any of it the next day. But if those ten pages contained a gripping true-life story of love and adventure, you might well be able to tell it to someone else a year later.

The difference, of course, would be that the story interested you and the statistical report didn't.

On the other hand, if you were a trained economist

and the report concerned your special field of study, it might be just the other way around. That wad of statistics might strike you as the most fascinating document since *Fanny Hill*.

It's the same way with the people you meet. If you find them interesting, you don't have to worry about remembering them. Their names and faces will stick in your memory a long time. If you *don't* find them interesting, that's when you have a problem.

But the difference is up to you.

Everyone is interesting if you'll just take the trouble to dig beneath the surface. Some of the world's greatest adventurers, outlaws, and *femmes fatales* resembled retired bank clerks or prim little old spinster ladies in their later years. To judge by his picture, Billy the Kid looked like an adenoidal high-school dropout. If Napoleon could have been transported from his place of exile on St. Helena to the streets of modern New York and disguised in present-day clothing, he would probably look like a potbellied little proprietor of a dry-cleaning shop who does alterations on a sewing machine in his back room.

Think what you'd be missing if you let yourself be put off by outward appearances and passed up such extraordinary specimens.

But when people don't volunteer any information about themselves, there's only one way to find out all this fascinating data—and that is to *ask*. Don't think they'll resent your nosiness, either. On the contrary, you'll generally find them eager to open up—and grateful to you for asking. Nothing is more flattering to the ego than an attentive audience listening avidly while we talk about ourselves.

What's more, your interest in them will tend to inspire a corresponding curiosity about *you*, and by now some degree of personal warmth is bound to start creeping into the relationship. This can be the beginning of true friendship. But only if you keep in mind . . .

THOUGHT NUMBER 4

Almost everybody's interesting and
worth adding to your power network
—once you get to know them

Once a friendship has sprouted and taken root, it needs to be cultivated, like a seedling plant.

You may not be able to water it daily, but you should certainly try to keep in touch at not-too-infrequent intervals—by phone, letter, or personal contact.

And, needless to say, keeping in touch should never take on the aspect of a duty call. Perhaps the best occasions are when you have news to pass along—preferably news of more importance to your friend than to you. The very fact that you took the trouble to bring it to his or her attention is flattering proof of your high regard.

Moreover, the very nature of news tends to impart a certain chattiness to the conversation that makes it warm and friendly and natural.

Many people use birthday cards and holiday greetings as a way of keeping friendships in good repair. They certainly help. Even though Christmas cards and gifts have taken on a slightly mercenary, almost computerized aura these days, the recipient is still flattered to know that you regard him as important enough to be put on your Christmas list.

Speaking for myself, I find telephone calls the quickest, as well as the most personal and efficient, way to keep in touch with people whose acquaintance or friendship I value.

Whatever means of keeping in touch you use, it's important to remember . . .

THOUGHT NUMBER 5

Individual circuits of your power network should receive frequent signal testing

Obviously you'll be forming your private power network primarily for your own benefit—because you want to start a current of luck pulsing through it. And with the luck flowing toward *you*.

But remember, as Edison found out, direct current, which is one-way current, is of only limited use for the transmission of power.

Efficient, high-voltage power transmission can be achieved only with alternating (two-way) current, which flows through the circuit in both directions.

By the same token, if you want your power network to start generating luck really efficiently, remember that the luck must flow both ways.

For example, if you hear about a job opening that might be just right for one of your network contacts, get on the horn and tell him about it pronto.

If a friend will soon be moving into town and you get wind of an imminent apartment vacancy, tip him off.

Someone you know has just landed in the hospital for an unpleasant operation? Don't wait until he gets out to sympathize. Send him a card or a gift of fruit right now. Better yet, call him, if possible, and ask if there are any chores or errands you can attend to for him while he's laid up in the hospital.

Believe me, someday—maybe not tomorrow, but

someday (to paraphrase the old song)—those favors and acts of thoughtfulness will be returned to you tenfold.

There's no doubt at all about that in my mind. I've seen it happen too often. I really believe it's a law of nature.

Every time you do so, you're recharging your luck-making circuits! So file this away in your mind as . . .

THOUGHT NUMBER 6

To keep a current of luck flowing
through your power network,
care about your contacts

Let me close this chapter with one more example to illustrate just how effectively a power network can operate in *generating luck*.

Recently I was invited to attend a biorhythm conference in Edinburgh, Scotland. The organizers of the conference want me to deliver a lecture and also participate in a seminar. I have accepted, and when the conference is over, you may be sure that I'll write a personal letter to everyone I met there. I also called my British publisher to alert him to the conference for publicity purposes and to arrange for a supply of my biorhythm books to be made available for sale and autographing. During our phone conversation he asked what new projects I was working on; and when I told him I was writing a new book on biorhythm, he immediately expressed interest in obtaining the British rights.

Next day I received an urgent call from a women's magazine in England, inquiring about the possibility of magazine serialization of my new book. The magazine editor, as it turned out, had learned about my book from the last book-publishing convention in Frankfurt. I thought the magazine was owned by a big German publisher, one of whose top executives happened to be in New York at this time. I was asked to contact him for further talks. At the moment he was in the process of developing a brand-new women's weekly magazine here in the United States, and he immediately became interested in obtaining the American magazine rights to my book—on- top of which, after learning about my other activities, he bought an astrology feature and a biorhythm article for his new magazine.

Does that give you some notion of the tremendous potential of a power network for generating luck?

Your own power network can do the same for you.

13

Ready, Set, Go

*I*n Dickens' novel *Great Expectations* there's a dotty old lady living in a moldering mansion. The dining table in the mansion is spread for a lavish wedding feast that never came off because her suitor jilted her at the last moment.

And now the table is overlaid with dust and cobwebs, nibbled at by mice and rats. Eventually the candlesticks get knocked over, the tablecloth catches fire, and both the mansion and the old lady go up in flames.

I'm always reminded of this sad story whenever I meet anyone (and there are plenty of such people) who's full of brilliant ideas for achieving success—but never does anything about them.

That person jilts himself out of success by failing to act on his daydreams.

Everything you've learned from this book so far is worthless unless and until you start putting your ideas into action right now—today.

Yes, I know, I know. I've told you that several times

in the course of the past twelve chapters—each time trying to nudge you into action.

Now you tell *me* something: Have I succeeded so far?

Have you taken a single step yet toward making your own luck? If the answer is yes, then I feel absolutely confident that you're already halfway toward your goal of raising yourself from your present level of humdrum, stick-in-the-mud existence to a newer, happier, more successful way of life.

Believe me, there's nothing all that difficult about achieving your goal. God gave you eyes, ears, hands, nose, and a brain to think with—what more do you need? All you have to do is use them. Even without a full quota of limbs or normal faculties, many people have achieved outstanding success, as we've seen. Their only secret was grit, determination, common sense, and hard work.

If you'll go back and analyze everything I've told you so far, you'll know by now that all luck boils down to those same simple ingredients.

No, there's nothing difficult about making your own luck and achieving your goal of success. The truth is, it's quite easy. Just try, and you'll soon find out for yourself exactly how easy it is. You don't even need me to tell you how. The answers are already programmed into your normal instincts.

If you fall in the water, do you need an instruction book or an educational cassette to advise you that your first priority must be to try to stay afloat and, as soon as possible after that, to yell for help?

Of course not. Anytime you feel you're in danger of drowning, your instinct of self-preservation takes over. From there on, you just do what comes naturally.

The same law holds true with achieving success. Once you've set your sights on a definite goal, all you have to do is let your instincts take over—and listen to the voice of common sense. It'll translate anything your instincts are trying to tell you into simple, easy-to-follow steps.

Very likely you've seen one of those exciting movies about fighting men in World War II escaping from stockades, concentration camps, or POW camps. Do you recall any sequences in such films showing the prisoners studying a manual titled "How to Escape in Ten Easy Lessons" or "A Layman's Guide to Tunnel Digging"?

Foolish question.

Escaping from prison camp doesn't require any four-year course of postgraduate study or any high-priced, specially designed spades or pickaxes, either. Those escapees use any sort of makeshift tools they can lay hands on, including broken spoons, and just start scratching away at the ground for all they're worth until they're on the other side of that barbed wire.

At all times, such real-life escapees relied on gut instinct and common sense to guide them, and this is exactly the same way you or I or anyone else goes about the business of making our own luck.

As a matter of fact, I can see striking similarities between success strivers and escaping prisoners of war.

Both have to break out of their own special kinds of *confinement.*

In the case of a prisoner of war, that confinement takes the form of barbed wire, armed guards, attack dogs, and so on.

In *your* case, it means breaking out of a tight circle of habit, fear, lethargy, doubt, laziness—all the set ways of thinking and acting (or *not* acting) that have kept you mired in a rut, out of reach of satisfying success and prideful achievement.

And once you do break out of confinement, you still have a long way to go before you're home free.

Don't get me wrong when I tell you it's easy. It doesn't mean you won't have to work your heart out or won't encounter any problems, obstacles, disappointments, setbacks, and other assorted pains in the neck, any more than those escaping war prisoners got safely home without facing all sorts of dangers and hardships.

But think of the sheer exhilaration once you're off and running on the road to your goal.

What I really mean when I tell you it's easy to make your own luck and achieve success is that there's no mystery to it. Anyone can figure out how it's done once he puts his mind to it.

What's hard is getting started and keeping at it.

Let's go back for a moment to that question I asked earlier in this chapter: Have you taken a single step yet toward making your own luck?

If the answer is no, then why not? What's stopping you? Is it sheer laziness? Somehow I doubt that. A truly lazy person probably wouldn't be much interested in success in the first place—or, at any rate, not enough to read a whole book about it.

More likely any apparent laziness is due to the kind of psychological fatigue described by that famous philosopher and classical scholar Mortimer Adler. In a magazine article titled "Success Means Never Feeling Tired," Adler explains how such fatigue can actually arise from the experience or fear of failure.

When we think a job will prove too tough for us to handle, we become reluctant to tackle it. Our reluctance makes us feel tired before we even start; and the more tired we feel, the more convinced we become that the job will prove too tough for us, which in turn makes us feel even more reluctant to start and therefore more tired than ever— a vicious circle.

Adler offers three suggestions for breaking out of this trap:

1. Recognize that your tiredness is mental, not physical, and therefore resting or postponing won't help; when the time comes to tackle the job tomorrow, you'll feel just as tired then as you do now.

2. So put on your thinking cap and figure out the best way to do whatever has to be done; and let the problem germinate in your mind long enough for your subconscious to come up with whatever brilliant strokes of inspiration it can offer.

3. Then apply your willpower and plunge ahead.

Once you break through this crippling barrier of psychological fatigue, you'll find your energy flowing stronger than ever. This is when you'll find yourself putting in twelve- to sixteen-hour days and enjoying every minute of it, in the sheer thrill and exuberance of making full use of all your God-given powers.

This is what Adler means when he says that success means never feeling tired.

Or, to quote what I call Gittelson's Law: *The harder you work, the luckier you get.* (I doubt if I coined the phrase, but I do believe it.)

There's another kind of fear of starting that has nothing to do with the real or imagined difficulties of a given project. Quite the contrary—this is a *fear of success.*

If that sounds incredible, let me tell you that there are any number of well-known cases of this on record. Two that immediately come to mind were young authors back in the 1940s who wrote best-selling novels that became hit movies. With fame and fortune assured, and money pouring in, both Ross Lockridge, author of *Raintree County*, and Thomas Heggens, creator of *Mister Roberts*, committed suicide—at the very peak of success.

Don't ask me why. I'm not a psychiatrist. Presumably success tends to confront such people with terrifying problems and temptations that they're simply not able to cope with.

There are also *masochistic* types who don't so much fear success; rather, they enjoy failure. If they do accidentally become successful, they take to drink or squander their money or antagonize everyone by such outrageous behavior that they soon wind up falling flat on their faces again. This seems to be a common syndrome among Hollywood movie stars who, as the saying goes, "let success go to their heads."

If you really think you fall into one of these categories, then of course the wisest thing to do may be to seek psychological counseling.

Let me hasten to add that I personally doubt very much that you're suffering from either syndrome. As a matter of fact, while writing this book I sought opinions on the subject from two psychiatrists. Both stated as their belief that neither masochists nor success fearers were likely to be found boning up on how to make their own luck.

My own hunch is that if you're still stalling at this point, it's because you're looking through the wrong end of the telescope and shrinking your own horizons—all because of two common misconceptions, which I call the *paycheck delusion* and the *never-can-be fallacy*.

If you can overcome these two obstacles, you'll be giving a strong booster charge to your luck-making battery.

Let me explain what they are and what you can do about them.

* * *

THE PAYCHECK DELUSION

E. Joseph Cossman is a self-made millionaire. He's not only a mail-order genius (*Ant Farm, Shrunken Head, Fly Cake, Art Masterprints*), he's the author of two best-selling books, an inspirational lecturer, and at last report the operator of a projected chain of franchised Cossman Future Millionaire Clubs, which will show ambitious people how to develop, market, and promote new products of their own creation.

Joe is a wellspring of choice quotes that invariably hit the nail right on the head, but the one I like best is from his book *Self-Made Millionaires:*

A weekly paycheck is not security—it's a handicap.... Too many of us have "salaryitis", and when that happens ingenuity goes out the window. I think it's one of the greatest evils in the U.S. When a man is given a salary, he's afraid to risk it, and the American educational system compounds the problem.

Education in this country is almost totally programmed to producing people to work as employees for someone else. It turns budding entrepreneurs into corporation employees. The man who strikes out on his own is a dying breed.

Truer words were never spoken. I couldn't have said it better myself, so I won't even try.

There's only one point on which I'd be inclined to differ with him. Joe seems to imply that Americans are merely *swayed* toward this paycheck addiction by the education they receive in the public schools; in other words, that without this mass-educational influence, they would naturally be more inclined toward economic self-reliance.

Well, maybe so. But it seems to me the situation is even more critical than he realizes.

Personally I would estimate that far more than half of

all Americans—perhaps as many as two-thirds—regard a paycheck existence as the normal way of life. As often as not, they absorb their parents' outlook on such matters. If their father brought home a weekly paycheck to feed and support the family, they'll tend to assume that they should do the same.

I believe that Americans can now be divided into two groups: (1) those who, on finishing school or college, plan to seek employment in some company or branch of government, and (2) those who think in terms of *making money*— by themselves and for themselves.

I'm sure you can guess which side I'm on. To me it's amazing to read and hear the endless hot air that gets written and spoken—especially in an election year—about the sturdy old American virtues of hard work and self-reliance when, in point of fact, the vast majority of people at both ends of that stream of hot air have no idea or experience of how to make money on their own, and would panic if faced with the prospect of doing without that security blanket called a paycheck.

I wonder if they realize that most of those pioneers they claim to admire so much, who came across the ocean to face a life of hardship and danger in an unknown land, or struck out into the wilderness to carve out homesteads for their family; that those same pioneers were, by and large, individuals who would have scorned to be another man's wage slave—their whole motivation in life was to make themselves truly independent and able to tell anyone they didn't like to go jump in the lake.

Recently we had a President who scornfully denounced those Americans who sought cradle-to-the-grave security from Big Brother. The only real security in this life, he loved to thunder, was the kind you get in the poorhouse.

All this sounded thrillingly impressive until you

stopped to reflect that, literally from his teens, he himself had spent his whole life on the public payroll, basking in the security of a regular government paycheck.

Sorry, I didn't mean to get carried away. My only reason for making such a big deal of what Joe Cossman calls "salaryitis" is that your attitude on this subject can make a big difference when it comes to making your own luck.

If you've spent your whole life fully convinced that only an employer has the power to make money flow into your hands, then it's often very difficult to get it through your head that you yourself have this same magic power—if you'll only use it.

And this may be the reason you're finding it so hard now to get off dead center and start making your own luck.

What to do about it?

I believe the solution lies in *proving to yourself* that you can make money by experimenting with a few small-scale preliminary tests. For instance:

1. Next Saturday afternoon, have a small garage sale, or take some unwanted household item that's still in usable condition—say a piece of furniture that's been relegated to the basement or attic—and offer it for sale through a want ad or supermarket bulletin board.

2. Offer your services in some capacity (never mind how humble; this is only an educational experiment), such as tutoring or baby-sitting or by putting your power mower in the car trunk and driving around to solicit lawn-cutting work—or even by renting a truck and taking on a couple of small hauling jobs.

3. Buy an old-model jalopy for not more than a hundred dollars, then fix it up a bit and try to sell it for more than you've invested. Don't worry about getting stuck with it—high-school kids are always looking for cars of this vintage.

I hope that a bit of money-making experience on this limited scale may help to convince you—or at least *start* to convince you—that you, too, can acquire some of that Midas touch that you always believed was reserved only for that remote, godlike being known as Your Employer.

From here you can go on to bigger things.

Remember, as Joe Cossman says: "Anyone in this country can make money if they aren't afraid to gamble on their own ability—if they refuse to settle for security alone—if they have the guts to dream and will work to make that dream a reality."

THE NEVER-CAN-BE FALLACY

Another psychological hazard that can hypnotize a person into failure is the *inability to believe* that he can ever be a success.

Oh, sure, he may be able to accept the idea in theory, to believe that other "little people" may somehow learn to make their own luck. But deep down in his heart of hearts he just cannot convince himself that he, too, has that awesome ability to become successful.

It can happen to other people, maybe, but not to him.

Is it ever possible to root out such a deep-seated attitude?

Yes, I believe it is, once you've identified the problem.

Back in the 1920s a popular way of coping with such hang-ups was the Emile Coué method (named after the Frenchman who invented it) of saying to yourself, over and over, some such mantra as "Every day in every way I'm getting better and better."

If you think that method may work for you, by all means try it. There's ample evidence that it did work for a good many people.

In the final analysis, however, I believe that an ounce

of proof (such as that one picture people are always talking about) is worth a thousand words.

Therefore I suggest you try the same three experiments I suggested for exposing the paycheck fallacy, namely: (1) Try holding a garage sale, (2) offer your spare-time services, and (3) buy something cheap, such as an old jalopy, and sell it with a markup.

Again, one of these experiences (or something similar) may give you that added little bit of confidence to go on to the next step.

Or if a lucky rabbit's foot or some other lucky talisman will help, use that, too. This certainly seems to be a favorite method used by professional athletes to boost their confidence, so who knows? There may be something to it.

Okay, so you're finally ready for the acid test. It's graduation day and you're all set to apply what you've learned in this book.

What now?

That, of course, will depend on your present situation and exactly how you hope to use your luck-making know-how.

Here are six typical cases and my suggestions as to the best strategy for each:

1. *A salaried company employee, stuck in a blind-alley job, who wants to get out of his rut and earn a raise or promotion.*

I would advise that, as a first step, you write what I call a White Paper stating the exact goal you hope to acomplish within your company. Your basic mechanism for achieving this goal, of course, will be to convince your boss that you've earned such a reward.

How? . . . By first giving him something of such value that it will be only natural for him to respond in kind.

Presumably you've worked in his office or department

for some time. Therefore you must be well acquainted with all the faults and slipshod practices that are being perpetuated, day after day, in the office procedure. Put all these down in your White Paper.

For example, what waste-motion paperwork is being done that serves no useful purpose at all?

Just in my own office the other day, I found that one of the clerks was patiently copying down all the personal data on every customer who responded to one of my mail-order projects. Yet all these data were automatically going into our computer's memory bank when it responded to the customer's order.

I hate to think of the total number of hours and days that had been wasted in such totally useless work before I happened to discover her goof, quite by chance.

But to go on with your analysis: How can the flow of office work be smoothed to go faster and more efficiently? What is the overall purpose of your office or department and how can this be achieved more effectively? What procedures, if any, are long out of date and could be taken over by machine? What rewards or incentives could be introduced to increase the output of the employees? How could this office or department be made to play a larger, more productive role within the company as a whole?

Obviously, in undertaking such a bootstrap effort, you must be prepared to face the possibility of a smug, self-satisfied, incompetent, lethargic, or insecure-defensive department head or boss who may have no interest in improving his office procedures; he may be actively hostile to your suggestions because he sees you as a threat to his own tenure.

What to do in such a case?

The ball's now in your court again. It may be that this will crystallize your own feeling that the job is a total blind alley and dead end, not worth keeping—in which case, skip ahead to Number 5. Or it may decide you to apply for a transfer to another job within the company that offers greater opportunity for advancement.

2. *A housewife whose children are grown, who wants to enter or reenter the business world.*

Again, the first step is a White Paper laying out all the facts.

What are your skills? What type of work would you prefer to do? What companies in your area offer this kind of work? If it's a part-time position you're looking for, what hours of the day and what days of the week are you available?

There are many companies today that have jobs or work that require only part-time personnel, so they are actively interested in finding people just like you. So your problem is basically one of *making contact*, which in turn means making your availability known to employers who may be looking for someone just like you.

Referring back to the basic luck-making procedure, think of yourself as the new product you're trying to merchandise.

Gather all the information relevant to your marketing problem. Then start making contact—by studying the want ads, by making phone calls, by writing letters, by placing an ad in your local paper, by advertising your services on the supermarket bulletin board.

3. *A wage earner who wants to start his own business.*

As we've learned in the preceding chapters, your beginning point here will be an *idea*. Obviously this idea should reflect the type of work or field of activity you would like to be in.

Your first impulse may be to go for a franchise. But be very cautious here. In some cases a franchise may represent an excellent business opportunity. But, more often than not, they represent only generalized opportunities that may be only approximately suitable for your specific location and interest. Moreover, they often require sizable investments that can be lost before you know what hit you.

You may be better off with a clever, well-thought-out idea of your own, especially if it can be tried out at first on a spare-time basis and out of your own home, with no initial outlay of capital.

In any case, get all the possible advice you can *before* taking the plunge. Don't hesitate to question other people in the same line of business, and don't be afraid that they will turn you away rudely or suspiciously as a possible future competitor. So long as you don't open your business in the same community, they won't regard you as competition at all. And more than likely, they'll be flattered that you've come to them for advice and be only too happy to talk shop and share the fruits of their own experience. Such advice *beforehand* can save you countless costly mistakes and hundreds or thousands of dollars of wasted capital.

Don't worry that a part-time venture will overload you with work or prevent you from giving it your best efforts. I happen to be the proud owner of a beautiful rush-bottom chair, crafted in a Colonial American design. The chair bears the signature of its maker—*Eleanor Roosevelt*. She not only founded the business that made such furniture, but actually found time to work in the shop herself—and all this during one of the busiest periods in her life, when her husband, FDR, was governor of the state of New York.

4. *A female office worker or store clerk, trapped in a stereotyped job role, who wants to get into more venturesome work but has no marketable skills.*

Shyness and lack of experience in the male-dominated business world are likely to be your biggest handicaps. But they need not be serious. Decide at the very beginning what type of work will be most to your liking, then learn absolutely all there is to know about it and how to demonstrate effectively whatever it is you have to offer. These two factors will help to give you the confidence you need and will also go a long way toward winning the respect of your male colleagues or clients.

Basically you'll be selling either a product or service, as well as your own unique personality and talents. So the *idea-contact-circuit* procedure for luck-making will apply all the way.

5. *A business executive who has always been on salary in a large corporation but now yearns to found a business of his own.*

Almost certainly the biggest mental obstacle to be overcome will be your fear of failure. All your life you have worked within the secure framework of a successful company, and now you are contemplating exposing yourself and your family to the risks of a brand-new undertaking. No one but you can weigh the alternatives one against the other—the enjoyment of your present hard-won status as a successful corporation executive versus the thrill, satisfaction, and possibly greater financial rewards of running your own business.

Precisely because you have such a weighty decision to make, my advice would always be to try it on a moonlighting basis first. True, this may involve you in a heavy workload for the time being, but it will also protect your family from much of the risk you would otherwise be taking in an all-or-nothing plunge.

You may also find yourself facing the question of whether or not to take a partner. There will always be people eager to get a piece of a good thing or to get in on the ground floor of a promising new venture. Partners can provide additional capital and extra "hands," both of which can hasten your growth.

But any partnership is fraught with the same complicated problems of adjustment and cooperation as a marriage. A partnership that leads to wrangling and disharmony can hasten your failure just as surely as a good one can hasten your success. And if your partner turns out to be a sharpy, there's always the danger you may wind up on the outside of a deal that you originally started.

If you can do without a partner and his additional investment in your enterprise, I suggest that you do so. Run with your ideas with all your strength and capital, so that you are in full control. And if it should turn out that further capital is needed, then try to sell only a minority interest so that you remain in control.

6. *A retired senior citizen who wants to augment his slender pension and Social Security income.*

In many ways you are in a highly favorable operating position. You have much to offer any employer—not only in specific skills but in mature wisdom and business experience. Moreover, you can probably be more flexible in your working hours than any other type of employee. And your general reliability, stability, and sense of responsibility tend to be superior to those of all other categories of workers.

Your procedure for finding employment will generally be the same as that of a housewife entering or reentering the job market.

Should you decide to go into business for yourself, you will naturally have to be most careful of your limited capital—more so than most younger people. On the other hand, you are also likely to be far more aware of the pitfalls of business.

I would advise you to embark on any independent business venture only on a strictly limited basis in the beginning—take one step and one deal at a time. When you are on Social Security, your tax situation is affected when your earned income reaches a certain level. Check with your accountant or local Social Security office.

By now I hope I have convinced you that luck can be manufactured *by* yourself *for* yourself.

Once you make up your mind that you want to go ahead, put up your antenna, put on your receivers, open your eyes—and start becoming aware of the needs of the market all around you. It will be as obvious as the missing-tooth space in the smile of Leon Spinks.

Select those markets that your own talents will let you step into, even if you need a little help. But if you have a feeling—a gut reaction—that with a little bit of training or help you can make it, then *start today*.

Not tomorrow, *now*.

And always remember: A good idea is only a *think* away, and success is only an *act* away.

14

The Time Is Now

*I*n this book I have tried to give you the boiled-down essence of a lifetime of experience in the world of business—so that you, too, can *make your own luck*.

I wonder how well I have succeeded.

I ask myself, in fact—and not for the first time—how well qualified I am to have undertaken such a task in the first place.

Only you can be the judge.

My background is at least well rounded.

If I haven't made a billion dollars, as Armand Hammer has, I have certainly made more money than the average businessman.

If I haven't yet been to the moon, my business ventures have, nevertheless, taken me to every corner of the world.

And, Lord knows, they have embraced a mind-blowing variety of products and services, ranging from military tanks to desk diaries, from advising governments to casting computerized horoscopes.

The *luck-making principles* I have culled from all this are remarkably simple.

In essence, I suggest that you . . .

• Look for a lucky idea.

> What makes an idea lucky is that it offers a new, better way to satisfy people's needs or desires. Such ideas are all around you if you keep your antenna up at all times.

• Do something about your idea promptly.

> Namely, do something that will help you start turning it into reality.

• Check out your idea *thoroughly*.

> Take nothing for granted. Gather all the information you need from the people who know most about the subject. Test your idea experimentally, if only by asking questions, to make sure people really *want* and *will pay* for whatever it is you plan to offer them.

• Make a connection.

> Get in touch with any person or persons who can aid your efforts to get your idea off the ground.

• Lay out your circuit.

> Proceed step by step—and as cheaply as possible at the start—to cover all the bases necessary to get your idea from the "raw material" stage into the hands of the final consumer.

• Turn on the juice.

> Carry out your idea in the actual marketplace.

• Build an ever-expanding network.

> Seek out friends and contacts who can help you make this idea pay off and generate *more luck* in the future.

Boiled down still further into a *single luck-making principle*, I would advise you to *look for ways to help other people*.

The wonderful thing about this principle is that it can be applied effectively and with amazing results in any situation, which includes:

- improving your job status
- starting and running your own business
- making your personal life happier

To state the same principle in still another way, I would also advise you to *give generously of yourself at all times*.

Don't worry about people taking advantage of you or about being made a sucker just through practicing this philosophy. That kind of attitude is for small-minded worry warts.

In any case, I'm not talking about giving away your hard-earned money to any sponger who asks for a handout. I'm talking about giving something far more important—namely, *yourself*, in the form of your personal warmth and interest and advice—to your friends or customers or business associates or other fellow humans whenever you're in a position to render them a helpful service.

I can assure you from long experience that, for reasons best known to the good Lord, if you make a regular habit of doing this, you will always get back far more than you give.

What you do with the luck-making principles I've tried to impart is up to you.

One thing is certain: Nothing will happen, and no luck will result, unless and until *you yourself do something*.

If you've grown up imbued with the notion that you must look to other people for employment and a paycheck, it may be very hard to accept the counter-idea that *you can make your own luck*—meaning money, fame, success, happiness—in short, that you can *succeed by your own efforts* in achieving whatever you want out of life.

But it's a fact. And all it takes to prove it is one successful effort on your part. From such efforts, step by step, will come all the confidence you need.

If you've also grown up convinced that power lies in numbers, I ask you to discard that fallacious idea, too, and accept the fact that *one* is the majority, *one* is the power.

History relates, beyond any doubt, how often the world has been changed for better or worse by the thoughts or efforts of a single human being, whether that person be Jesus, Napoleon, Einstein, Bach, Hitler, or Roosevelt—or the first man who made a hamburger.

We as humans have the seeds and potential to make or break a life, a business, a community, a city, a country.

Whether or not we develop this ability, and what use if any we make of it, depend on many things, such as genes, environment, need, persistence, training, lust, ideals, and greed. All these factors and many more exist as influences solely within ourselves.

To the extent that the ability develops, it yields many seeds. Only a fraction of them may germinate, yet the potential existed in each and every one.

Seeds, of course, have no control over their destiny. But people do.

This power we possess can be as mighty as an atom bomb. Most people scarcely realize this. They grow only a little or only at someone else's urging—not realizing that this power of growth has always existed inside them, whenever they wish to make use of it.

Many of us are so humble or intimidated that we feel helpless. The odds seem so large, the chances of success so small. "And besides," they ask plaintively, "how can we get started?"

The truth is that the world all around us is full of opportunities, not just sometimes but *all* the time, just as the ocean is always full of fish. One must simply start fishing.

It's rare that a fish will just jump into one's boat, although I'm sure that that has happened. But I wouldn't want to wait for my next dinner solely on the hope of such good luck. Would you?

One person can start a revolution, as well as one person can stop it.

By the same token, you as an individual have the power and the opportunity to achieve success—if you want it badly enough. Enough, that is, to go out and seek it aggressively.

Success is always waiting for you—so go and claim it.

The human being is programmed with the ability to think, observe, come to conclusions, and select entirely on his own volition, not by chance.

The theory that a person must be there in the right place at the right time is true. *What is left out is the fact that practically every day of his life he was in the right place at the right time—only he wasn't aware of it, so the opportunity slipped by.*

Remembering only the times he *was* aware, he calls such occasions his "lucky day" or the day his life changed.

It doesn't take genius or being born with great wealth and power to succeed. What it takes is receptivity and the will to go forward.

Take such cases as a sixteen-year-old boy who raises scorpions for a living, or a twenty-five-year-old biologist who develops a market for raising and selling tadpoles, or a retired widower who becomes a priest at seventy-eight, or an anesthesiologist who learns of a photo-finishing machine that develops color prints within an hour and builds a successful chain of One Hour Photo Developing Centers. All are examples of individuals who were able to change their lives for the better regardless of age or experience or education—and thus enjoy the sweet taste of success and achievement, capped by the glorious feeling that they "did it."

That feeling of accomplishment is what makes living worthwhile—what enables us to feel significant and important, even if only to ourselves.

To use an internal-combustion engine as an analogy, our self-regard provides the fuel, the action we take brings about the combustion, and the result is the progress or success we achieve.

We are born with all the faculties we need to succeed, so why not use them? Surely it's better to keep on trying to make our lives more fulfilling and satisfying, knowing that by doing so we are contributing in some small measure to human progress and thus individually counting in the story of mankind, and even more surely benefiting ourselves by our own efforts.

That, after all, is what makes life fun. That's why at times we can work twenty-four hours a day out of sheer drive and exuberance, lift twice our weight, and begin to use at least a portion of the vast, untapped power we all possess.

One person may look at a beautiful flower and be content to admire it. Another sees the same flower and tries to find a way to make a cutting so as to grow more such lovely blossoms. Still another sees the flower as a subject for a painting, or as scent for a perfume, or as a perfect work of nature to be copied in plastic, or believes it may have medicinal properties worth extracting and testing, or envisions it as the center of a charming floral arrangement.

Instead of just looking passively at the world around us, the point is to become aware of everything we see in relation to human needs and desires. All of us look, hear, see, and smell, but only those who peer behind the scenes, so to speak, and start to think of other possible uses or applications for what they see will end up with marketable products and successful achievements, or both.

This is what I mean by *making your own luck*.

Each example that I've cited in this book is comparable to a flower seen by many people—but out of all those who did, only one person went a thought further and became aware of the flower's other possibilities, thus starting the process that we call *luck*.

We produce luck only when we realize that Energy + Ideas = Results—and these results can become the bases of successful new business ventures.

Many years ago, while serving as an adviser to governments and corporations all over the world, I was often asked, "How can you advise a company in a country that you've never been to and whose customs and methods of doing business you know little about?"

My stock answer was that marketing and promotion are not unlike a doctor treating hypertension or obesity or any other health problem. There is no such thing as English cancer or Italian ulcers. The human organism is the same in any country, and so are the marketing and selling of merchandise. Aside from the necessity of having a license to practice in any given country, a good doctor could go into any hospital in the world and immediately start to do effective work. And the same principle holds true for a skilled marketing specialist. Certainly there may be a language problem, and some drugs or merchandising techniques may not be available everywhere or may be known under different names—but in both cases the procedure is basically the same all over the world.

Whatever country we may be in, business problems are the same—how to turn out a product that people need or can be persuaded that they need. Factories, too, in any country are always run for profit, by manufacturing goods and selling them for a price higher than cost—or trying to.

Employees, too, are the same the world over. They worry about layoffs and raises, fringe benefits and promotions. Corporate officers are no different. They struggle for power and fret that some newcomer may overtake and pass them on his way up the ladder. Even office politics and government politics are the same, with their universal infighting, back stabbing, lying, taking credit for things one had nothing to do with, while at the same time carefully avoiding any blame for failures, as long as one can get away with it.

By understanding and taking advantage of these universals of the business world, you can enhance your luckmaking ability and opportunities.

Praying that you will succeed by a miracle, such as saving the boss's life or marrying his daughter, is also a universal circumstance. These dreams and hopes are as common in Osaka as in Basel, in Marseilles or Düsseldorf as in Dallas. The nature of people in their fight for survival and achievement is the same the world over. And while some people may find it easier to make their own luck in one country than in another, I assure you I can find comparable success stories in every country—even in Communist countries.

The first time you discover you can float or swim by yourself, without sinking and inhaling a noseful of water, is like the first time you discover you can do something on your own in the business field. Now all you need is practice and technique.

The first time you try a new venture and succeed, you have proved to yourself that *you can do it*. Whether you sold your $500 frog for two $1,000 turtles, or sold your old $15 college textbook for $20, or decided to become a baby-sitter and got your first call, or became a store clerk and made your first sale—from that moment on, when you exclaim exultantly to yourself, *Yes, I can do it*, you will have entered a new world of achievement.

The next steps are simply to improve your technique and widen your venture.

As I write this I am in Brussels, where I came to meet a man who has just brought the right to my biorhythm computer system. After the business formalities we had a relaxed dinner, talking about current politics, the European Common Market, inflation, East versus West, and so on, and he told me his ambition was to write a book on a subject that he has been thinking of since he was six years old. "After I make some real money," he declared, "then I'll take the time to write the book—within three to five years, I hope."

"Frans," I said, "you're wrong. If you want to write that book, and it's been in your heart and dreams since you were six, start today—*now*. Start collecting books, articles, stories, and all sorts of facts that relate to the subject. Write a paragraph or a page every day and every week. Put them all in a box. Before you know it, the box will be full. Then you can start sorting, arranging, outlining, recognizing what else you need, and before you know it, you will have completed the research you need to sharpen your own ideas."

I drew some diagrams, illustrating a point I was making, showing the relationship of the individual to society.

"Take this scrap of paper," I said, "and let it be your start. I'll also mail you a copy of the book that Wendell Willkie wrote, called *One World*. That will start your bibliography. You can write that book, Frans, starting now—and still carry on your business."

He smiled and agreed—and I am willing to bet that he really will write his book. If he does, I will be rewarded with the knowledge that I inspired him by showing him how to stop dreaming and waiting for the day and to start carrying out his dream *now*.

John Erskine, who was an early president of the Juilliard School and a successful concert pianist, found time to write forty novels, yet still practiced two hours a day. When asked, "How do you do it?" he replied, "When you want to do something, you can *always* find the time—if you really want to."

I agree with all my heart, and I hope you will come to believe that as strongly as I do. In fact I want to encourage you to write me of your successes, so that in my books, lectures, and articles I will have more true-life anecdotes to pass along that may inspire others to make their own luck.

Recently three women—Susan O'Connell, thirty-four, executive secretary of a trucking company; Rachel Lyon, twenty-five, working in computer graphics; and Mindy Affrime, twenty-six, a travel agent—met and decided what they wanted most was to make a "big time" movie. They had little money, no script, no studio backing, and no cast. But they marshaled their efforts and went after the impossible, chipping in all they had for a major venture.

They decided to make a movie out of the book *Tell Me a Riddle*. But first they had to find the reclusive author in order to buy the rights to her work for seven-thousand dollars. Then they worked up a presentation and went around raising money, which none of them had ever done before. By calling and cajoling those on their list of prospects, they succeeded in convincing enough people that their movie project represented a worthwhile investment.

And at last the movie was made—for $1.2 million. The three onetime-amateur producers still don't know how they did it. But they found out one thing I've already spoken of earlier in the book—namely, how simple it often is to call important people. As Susan says, "Half the time all they're doing is sitting at their desks, hoping someone will call them with a good idea."

How true—believe me. There is always someone willing to listen to whatever you have to say and even to help. But you will find this out only by asking.

First get your luck-making idea by becoming more aware of the world and the people all around you. Tune in with all of your senses so that you will become sensitive to their needs and wants. Then start your venture.

You may fail on your first try. Many have done so, only to achieve a greater success than they dreamed of on their second try—or their third or fourth or fifth.

Imagine how many sketches and paintings Picasso turned out before he became the most successful and acclaimed artist of modern times. Yet he never regarded his early efforts as failures. They were experiences to learn from as he perfected his craft and technique.

Some of us may need more practice than others. Sometimes one's first sketch is perfect. But more often we must go through a process of putting down our idea on paper, reviewing and changing it, trying it unsuccessfully the first time, and finally going back to the drawing board for still more work and refinement.

If the great masters in art and science and business have had to succeed that way, why should we expect to be different?

The important lesson to be learned from all this is that the dream of "doing something someday" can come true only when we change *someday* to *today*. Someday is *now*.

I wish you well as you set out on your journey toward whatever goal you have chosen. I will share in the thrill of your success and cherish it personally as a very real reward in my own life.

MORE HELPFUL READING FROM *WARNER BOOKS*